CHRIST-FIGURES

Other Books by Peter Malone
published by Coventry Press

Hearts Burning Within Us
Dear Movies
10 Minutes: Gospel Reflections for Minds and Hearts

FINDING HUMANITY

Peter Malone MSC received an international award for the quality of his film criticism in 2021 and is a theological scholar of high repute. His scholarship and critical skills are amply evident throughout this very rewarding book.

In the book, he writes on 'Christ-figures' in movies ranging in time from 'On the Waterfront' (1954), through 'The Sound of Music' (1965), to 'Nomadland' (2020). Thirty movies are individually discussed and are drawn from a variety of genres to illustrate different styles of film-making and direction; and to address gender, cultural identity, and the passage of time. The book presents readers with a stimulating unmasking of how movies work, why they work, and what drives film critics to make the judgments they do.

Using the theoretical frameworks of theology and spirituality, the author cleverly adopts the mnemonic device of 'Christ-figure' to illustrate Christian cinema experience. Significantly, the book looks for humanity in what is seen and heard. What viewers see at first glance as horrific, comic, or abhorrent may cloak efforts (succeeding or failing) to project the human need to be better. As the book argues, cinema is the art of exposing humanity in all its forms, and film critics must consistently be alert to the variety of its manifestations.

This is an outstanding book by an inspiring scholar. Peter Malone's 'Afterthoughts', which conclude the book, provide an excellent, uplifting model for ecumenical film criticism, and the book is eminently suited to spiritual reflection, and thoughtful educational discussion.

PETER SHEEHAN AO,
Associate of Jesuit Media

For over 30 years, I have had the privilege of teaching religious education in Catholic schools. As our world becomes increasingly dominated by the visual, Peter's writing provides us with contemporary theological language and keen insight that unpacks depictions of Christ and Christ-like characters. His early books gave me clearer lens and better language when exploring images of Jesus with middle and senior school students and leading professional learning sessions with teaching staff. Peter is an engaging educator with a gentle wit and humour. But what particularly stands out for me as an educator is his thoughtful references to the influence of culture and changing religious sensibilities when he reflects upon the message of a particular film.

In this latest offering, Peter explores the more subtle 'Christ images' found in mainstream films and invites us to journey with him in his musings. I have found his bite-size chapters perfect length in this hectic world we inhabit but his insights are not bite-size! They invite us into a deeper appreciation of the message; and insights into filmic characters that are indeed Christ-figures. Peter's observations of finding pointers to the message and person of Jesus in unexpected places evidences the Ignatian principle of 'finding God in all things'. I highly recommend this thoughtful and engaging book that has helped me see Jesus in a variety of characters and narratives.

CHARLES WATT,
Deputy Principal: Faith and Mission
Genazzano College, Kew

Told in a down to earth, descriptive and with sometimes a humorous touch, Peter candidly takes the characters in movies and links them with the Gospel Jesus. This book is more than just film reviews. Peter has tremendous skill in retelling a movie without giving away any spoiler alerts. The focus is on the character that is portrayed, and their likeness to the actions of Christ.

The movies chosen by Peter display a wide range of issues, and you'll find many genres included (sci-fi, romantic, biographical, documentary, war).

Peter has highlighted the Jesus figure in some of my favourite movies, and now I have a whole new list for my 'to watch list'. Peter aptly parallels the character's actions, and Jesus' actions through reference to scripture passages and stories.

In my spirituality sessions, I often use movie themes to help convey and uncover some deeper messages; Peter has suggested these for deeper reflection, giving us another layer from which to see in-depth.

This book is significant, with its ability to suggest a movie with an inspirational character, in both olden movies and up to date ones. Thank you, Peter, for giving us a book that reminds us that 'each of us is called to be a Christ-figure in our lives'.

SR RITA MALAVISI,
National Chair
Director
Conference of Spiritual Directors Australia

―― GOSPEL VALUES IN FILM ――

CHRIST-FIGURES

―― THERE ON OUR SCREENS ――

―― PETER MALONE ――

COVENTRY
PRESS

Published in Australia by
Coventry Press
33 Scoresby Road
Bayswater VIC 3153

ISBN 9781922589200

Copyright © Peter Malone MSC 2022

All rights reserved. Other than for the purposes and subject to the conditions prescribed under the *Copyright Act*, no part of this publication may be reproduced, stored in a retrieval system, or transmitted in any form or by any means, electronic, mechanical, photocopying, recording or otherwise, without the prior permission of the publisher.

Scripture quotations are from the *Jerusalem Bible* copyright © 1966 by Darton Longman & Todd Ltd and Doubleday and Company Ltd.

Catalogue-in-Publication entry is available from the National Library of Australia
http://catalogue.nla.gov.au

Cover design by Ian James – www.jgd.com.au
Text design by Coventry Press
Set in EB Garamond

Printed in Australia

The images on the front cover of *Christ-figures* depict the following films

Cries and Whispers (1971)
The Miracle Worker (1962)
To Kill a Mockingbird (1962)
The Sound of Music (1965)
On the Waterfront (1954)
Star Wars (1977)
Storm Boy (1976)
Silkwood (1983)
Gorillas in the Mist (1988)
The Year of Living Dangerously (1982)
Boy Erased (2018)
Edward Scissorhands (1990)
Awakenings (1990)
Nomadland (2020)
A Beautiful Day in the Neighborhood (2019)
Free Guy (2021)

Contents

Foreword	11
INTRODUCING OUR THEME	13
Jesus, *The Last Temptation of Christ* (1988)	17
CHRIST-FIGURES, WOMEN, MEN	21
Father Barry, *On the Waterfront* (1954)	23
Annie Sullivan (and Helen Keller), *The Miracle Worker* (1962)	26
Atticus Finch, *To Kill a Mockingbird* (1962)	29
Maria (Maria von Trapp), *The Sound of Music* (1965)	32
Agnes, *Cries and Whispers* (1971)	34
Fingerbone, *Storm Boy* (1976)	37
Obi-Wan Kenobi, *Star Wars* (1977)	40
Karen Silkwood, *Silkwood* (1983)	43
Dian Fossey, *Gorillas in the Mist* (1988)	46
Babette, *Babette's Feast* (1988)	49
Dr Malcolm Sayer, *Awakenings* (1990)	52
Edward, *Edward Scissorhands* (1990)	55
Glenn Holland, *Mr Holland's Opus* (1955)	58

Sister Helen Prejean, *Dead Man Walking* (1995)   61

William Wilberforce, *Amazing Grace* (2006)   64

Irena Sendler, *The Courageous Heart of Irena Sendler* (2009)   67

Nelson Mandela, *Invictus* (2009)   70

Katniss Everdeen, *The Hunger Games* (2012)   74

Martin Luther King Jr, *Selma* (2014)   77

Desmond Doss, *Hacksaw Ridge* (2016)   80

Ruth Bader Ginsburg, *On the Basis of Sex* (2018)   83

Mr Rogers, *A Beautiful Day in the Neighborhood* (2019)   86

Madame Curie, *Radioactive* (2019)   90

Fern, *Nomadland* (2020)   93

CHRIST-FIGURES, MEN AND WOMEN TOGETHER   97

Augusto and Michaela Odone, *Lorenzo's Oil* (1992)   99

Eric and Patti Lomax, *The Railway Man* (2013)   102

Nancy and Marshall Eamons, *Boy Erased* (2018)   105

Guy and Milly (and Keys), *Free Guy* (2021)   109

Billy Kwan, *The Year of Living Dangerously* (1982)   112

AFTERTHOUGHTS   115

Foreword

PETER MALONE IS a pioneering figure who started work on cinematic Christ-figures long before the subject became fashionable and before it started to appear on the curriculum of modules on theology/religion and film at the beginning of the 21st century. I first encountered Peter's work when I was doing my own PhD on redemption and film in the late 1990s, and I was fascinated by the way he took a popular, imaginative film such as *Edward Scissorhands* (Tim Burton, 1990) and used it as a portal into a theologically enriching conversation about Christology and Christ-figures.

I had studied Christian ideas about the person of Christ as part of my undergraduate studies, yet it would never have occurred to me back in the early 1990s that one might be able to find ways of using film to enable us to learn about Christology or of reading Christology through the lens of popular film.

Since I first taught a module on religion at film, first in the University of Wales and then since 2004 at the University of Kent, I have made sure that Peter's *Movie Christs and Anti-Christs* has appeared on the course bibliography. The book has not always been the easiest to get hold of, yet it is a seminal text because it was written in such a clear fashion and contains so many insightful comments about why particular films might lend themselves to interpretation through a Christ-figure lens.

In the summer of 2021, it was an enormous privilege to finally get to meet Peter for an episode of a podcast that I host on Nostalgia. Inevitably, we talked in depth about Peter's work on Christ-figures and on the way in which such films reveal one's own understanding of Jesus himself. My own take on the subject is that, provided we have a clear set of criteria for determining why we should be looking at these sort of Christic, salvific and messianic resonances, then it is a really fertile topic for examination and allows us to ask searching questions about how we may be afforded the opportunity to learn more about Christ through film and film through Christ.

Along the way, Peter gives us an engaging and personal set of reasons for choosing the set of films that form the bedrock of this book. Many of them are films most of us have seen, with some of them (such as *The Sound of Music* and *Star Wars*) the kind of films we may have seen many times since childhood and which have impacted on us to a profound degree. Peter does justice to the films in their own right while also asking how and why they may be useful as dialogue partners for a discussion of the role they may play for faith as well as educational purposes in the classroom, university lecture theatre, church, seminary and the movie theatre.

Chris Deacy,
Reader in Theology and Religious Studies
Director
University of Kent

Introducing our Theme

Jane Goodall, the celebrated Englishwoman, pioneer in the study of African chimpanzees, living immersed with the animals themselves, looking back to the line of human ancestry and its various evolutionary stages, was the kick-start, so to speak, for embarking on this exploration of Christ-figures. She was in conversation with Meredith Lake on Radio National's *Soul Search*, reflecting on her work in Africa, commenting on science and religious awareness, on her own faith journey and the prospect of publishing a book on Hope at the age of 87 (in November 2021). I was reminded of Dian Fossey. And then it occurred to me that Jane Goodall and Dian Fossey, each in their life and work-commitment for understanding nature and our world, was something of a saviour-figure. So a Christ-figure.

Why not some more exploration of Christ-figures? And the tantalising question of candidates. Nelson Mandela immediately came to mind. But, this was almost in the middle of the night, and while the mind and imagination were whirring, it was time to go to sleep. It is now morning! Time to put down some thoughts.

I have been enjoying the exploration of Christ-figures in films for almost fifty years. My friend, Fr Fred Chamberlin, who established Australia's Catholic Film Office, used to remark that I saw Christ-figures everywhere (if only Fred could see one or two!). But, aren't we all, in own different ways, figures of Christ in our world?

During the 1980s, it seemed a good idea to write a book with brief chapters, 1000 words per chapter, 30 words synopsis introduction (and the luxury of having a film still for each chapter), illustrating the variety of Christ-figures in films. The publishers opted for a catchy title, *Movie Christs and Antichrists*. The chapters are still valid – it is just that the film examples end at 1986. *The Mission* was released as the book went to press, a period when we were discovering more and more Christ Liberator-figures. (I was able to have the blessing of amplifying some of this material in a book which focused on as many Jesus-films as I could discover – up to 2012, *Screen Jesus: Portrayals of Christ in Television and Film*. My friend, Maggie Roux, who wrote the introduction, had suggested the subtitle, *From Celluloid to Digital*, which indicated the developments in technology over more than 100 years. But, the American publishers preferred stating the rather bland 'Television and Film'.

I just checked on Amazon and both books are still there!

One of the key things to note, always, is that in appreciating a Christ-figure in film, this has not necessarily been the intention of the filmmakers (mostly not). It is in our recognising similarities between a central figure and the characteristics of the Jesus of the Gospels. And I've always liked to add that the figures and their resemblance must be both substantial and significant. A gangster making a quick sign of the cross before he is gunned down by the Mafia is not a Christ-figure!

One of the great values of recognising Christ-figures is the revelation to the film viewer about the particular characteristics of Jesus that they themselves value, why they are recognised, why they appeal, and so building up their own portrait of Jesus. To that extent, this kind of film-watching moves into the area of spirituality. Watching, recognising and naming Christ-figures, then, is important for an individual, but also for group watching and sharing, whether it be students at school, members of youth groups, adult education, parish prayer and discussion groups. It might be said that recognising and discussing Christ-figures in film is a significant religious education experience.

Hence this book. I have chosen thirty Christ-figures from significant films. The films can be watched, reflected on, discussed – views surfacing, aspects of faith discovered, faith shared.

As my imagination started spinning, listening to Jane Goodall, an immediate thought came to mind. The first Christ-figure to be considered in this book should be Jesus himself. In this sense: there have been many Jesus' films, and the term that is used is Jesus-Figure, Jesus presented in a realistic way, Jesus presented in a stylised way (and the realisation that many of the portrayals which we consider realistic are, in their way, more stylised than real, De Mille's *The King of Kings* for a start). These films declare that they are based on the Gospels, but they are, of course, interpretations of the Gospel portrait of Jesus.

However, *The Last Temptation of Christ* comes to mind, the Greek orthodox novelist, Nikos Kazantzakis, indicating that this was not a Gospel story as such. It was his meditation and expanded-imagination interpretation of Jesus. It meant that he created episodes that were not found in the Gospels. He created episodes that explored the psyche of Jesus, trying to deal with his humanity, his divinity, the demands of the incarnation and his mission. And in Martin Scorsese's film, 1988, there was the controversial hallucination sequence where Jesus is told by the angel that he has fulfilled his father's will and he can come down from the cross and lead an ordinary life.

When we come to think of it, many of the familiar Jesus-films also include sequences that were not in the Gospels, the filmmakers' interpretations of how Jesus might act in situations that they created in their screenplays. In more recent times, the popularity of the television series, *The Chosen*, which certainly included a great number of these sequences, reminds us that from the early church times with the Apocryphal Gospel narratives to the films and television series of the last hundred years, there is a yen in the human imagination and human heart for more stories of Jesus, our creating ever more Jesus Christ-Figures.

And so, on to other Christ-figures, men and women, Christian and characters who are not religious, but who, in real life or in fiction, have shown us how facets of Jesus' life – his words, his actions – have been reflected.

I hope that this book can be a creative start, spur, to spirituality and faith.

The Last Temptation of Christ (1988)

Jesus

WE ALL HAVE our own Jesus-figure. Or, rather, our Jesus-figure continues to change throughout our lives – our childhood image, whether we thought about him much or not in adolescence, our adult Jesus-figure as we faced significant questions in our lives, growth in faith, lessening faith, ongoing challenges. And there were our favourite Gospel passages – what Jesus said, what Jesus did, incidents that appeal to us, episodes that mystify us. And our Jesus-figure is a continuing, lifelong project.

Perhaps we could call our Jesus-figure a figure of faith. But it depends on what we mean by faith. Centuries ago, St Augustine wrote about different experiences of faith: there was belief in what God revealed as true – doctrinal and moral perspectives; there was faith that transferred into action, not only love of God but love of neighbour; then there was the faith that sustained us through our life and our belief in our ultimate destiny with God. When asked to describe that faith, it might emerge as our 'spirituality'.

But, when we reflect on our explorations of the person of Jesus, we realise that, in some ways, we have created our figure of Jesus, starting points with Gospel stories, continuing with our imagination of what Jesus might have been like. And so Jesus becomes our Christ-figure.

As suggested in the introduction, a challenging example of this kind of creation of Jesus/Christ-figure can be found in Nikos Kazantzakis' novel, *The Last Temptation of Christ*, screenplay by Paul Schrader (a Michigan Calvinist background), directed by

Martin Scorsese (a New York Catholic background). Quite an ecumenical venture in its way. The film looks like a Gospel film, even a version of the Gospel. But the author and filmmakers intended it as a fiction based on the Gospels. The kind of thing that we see these days in many films and television series: 'based on a true story, inspired by actual events'.

Watching and testing our response to *The Last Temptation* can be quite illuminating about our own spirituality, offering new perspectives on Jesus himself.

Kazantzakis downplays, so to speak, the divinity of Jesus. This was found very offensive for those who tend to up-play the divinity, sometimes wary of describing or talking about Jesus as human. This tension between Jesus' humanity and divinity (a profound theological issue in the early centuries of the church, leading to ecumenical councils, decisions and decrees, creeds, heresies and secession) has a kind of pendulum history, even during the 20th century, more emphasis on the divinity in the first half, a growing emphasis on the humanity in the second half of the century.

This emerged in the response to Scorsese's film. There was a great deal of emphasis on Jesus agonising, tormented in himself about himself and his relationship with God.

At the time, some commentators noted the spiritual/theological sonnets by British poet, Gerard Manley Hopkins, like *Carrion Comfort*, where the poet experienced the torment of the mystery of his relationship with God. And other commentators noted that, twenty years earlier, in the television version of Dennis Potter's *Son of Man*, Colin Blakeley as Jesus was similarly tormented and a repeated piece of dialogue, an anguishly puzzled 'is it me?', 'Is it me?'... resembled the questions of Jesus' agony in the garden – and in popular culture, it is also echoed in the agony song, culminating in Jesus' primal scream before surrendering to the will of the Father, in *Jesus Christ, Superstar*.

Another aspect of Jesus' humanity that troubled some audiences at the time but found favourable comment by others is Jesus' friendship with Mary Magdalene. The novelist and filmmakers have created Christ-figure aspects of Jesus, his knowing Mary from childhood, his support of her, even waiting for her at the brothel to help, affection for her (not always a word used in connection with Jesus), even taking a stone from angry accusers before they cast them at Mary for her sins.

The main sequence in the film where novelist and filmmakers create their Christ-figure is that of the crucifixion. It was here that the film was denounced as blasphemous. Some of the comment indicated that the word 'temptation' always has sexual connotations. Defenders of Kazantzakis were quick to point out that the last temptation is actually the temptation to give up on the mission that has been asked of us for life, the temptation to ordinariness.

And that is key to the crucifixion scene. The angel comes to Jesus, bereft and naked on the cross, telling him that he has obeyed God's command, has met the test, can now come down from the cross and go on his ordinary way. Some missed the fact that this sequence is a hallucination. Jesus does come down from the cross, does resume an ordinary life, in fact marries, is widowed, marries again, retires to Nazareth, the years passing, an ordinary, even mundane life. But, even in the hallucination, an angry Paul comes to Nazareth to upbraid Jesus, telling him that he has been preaching Christ crucified, so what is he doing in Nazareth. And then the apostles arrive, Jesus weak, ageing, being told that they expected him to be on the cross.

And he wakes. He is on the cross. He has not succumbed to the last temptation to give up on his mission. He can surrender to the father, giving himself completely in death.

We can remember that more mainstream Jesus films do this kind of Christ-figure exploration, creating stories, imagining what Jesus might have been like, what he might have done.

Christ-figures, women, men

On the Waterfront (1954)

Father Barry

ONE OF THE INTERESTING and challenging experiences in watching and reviewing films over many years is discovering how many movie characters are Catholic priests. Many more than I first imagined. Which then became a preoccupation, trying to discover and make notes on every representation of Catholic priests on the screen, leading to a rather large volume, *Screen Priests*. And it continues.

Priests began to make their appearance on screen in the 1930s – Spencer Tracy three times, including twice as Father Flanigan of *Boys Town*, Pat O'Brien dealing with gangsters in *Hell's Kitchen*... Of course, there was Bing Crosby and Barry Fitzgerald, *Going My Way* in the 1940s. These were genial priests, confident in their vocation, reaching out to people in need, exemplary in their way. From the 1960s, especially with *The Cardinal*, 1963, screened for bishops and clergy during the second session of Vatican II, priest characters became more complex, outreach yes, but doubts, problems with authority, different perspectives on church, and over the last decades, abusers. But priests should be Christ-figures.

One of the key phrases associated with Pope Francis and his comment on priests and priestly ministry is that they should be out there, not hidden away in sacerdotal seclusion, taking refuge in clericalism, out there 'with the smell of the sheep'. Father Barry, Karl Malden's character in *On the Waterfront* was out there, with the smell of labourers on the New York docks. His key scene is a sermon, a challenge, a confrontation with oppressive bosses, quoting Jesus and the crucifixion. He is in the church basement, talking. interacting with some of the workers after a brutal death:

'Boys, this is my church! And if you don't think Christ is down here on the waterfront, you've got another guess coming! Some people think the Crucifixion only took place on Calvary. They better wise up! Taking Joey Doyle's life to stop him from testifying is a crucifixion. And dropping a sling on Kayo Dugan because he was ready to spill his guts tomorrow, that's a crucifixion. And every time the Mob puts the pressure on a good man, tries to stop him from doing his duty as a citizen, it's a crucifixion. And anybody who sits around and lets it happen, keeps silent about something he knows that happened, shares the guilt of it just as much as the Roman soldier who pierced the flesh of our Lord to see if he was dead. Christ is saying with all of you, if you do it to the least of mine, you do it to Me!'

Father Barry makes Christ's passion and suffering alive for the hard labouring life of the waterfront.

In fact, Father Barry was based on an actual priest, a Jesuit, Father John M. Corridan. Screenwriter, Budd Schulberg, consulted him while writing the screenplay. The *Wikipedia* entry on Father Corridan quotes Schulberg (as well as highlighting the social change the priest achieved and his later teaching and chaplaincy ministries): Father Corridan, a 'tall, youthful, balding, energetic, ruddy-faced Irishman whose speech was a fascinating blend of Hell's Kitchen jargon, baseball slang, the facts and figures of a master in economics and the undeniable humanity of Christ'. And Schulberg's realisation of him as a Christ-figure: he 'led me to understand that there is nothing unusual about a Catholic priest's involving himself in moral issues that find practical form in the daily lives of his parishioners'.

On the Waterfront won the Oscar for Best Film of 1954. From the Catholic historical point of view, this is definitely pre-Vatican II. Looking back, many nostalgic, traditional Catholics yearn for those days – definition, clarity, obligations. Many enthusiastic-for-development Catholics, on the other hand, tend to underestimate, not appreciate the vitality in that pre-Vatican II church.

Father Barry represents the consciousness of Catholic social teaching of those years. Many go back to the late 19th century and papal and other documents, especially from Leo XIII in 1891, *Rerum Novarum,* on the significance of work and human dignity of workers. Twenty years or so before *On the Waterfront,* Pius XI, 1931, *Quadragesimo Anno* (on the 40th anniversary), reiterated and developed Catholic social teaching. In many parts of the world – Catholic Action in Europe, Canon Joseph Cardijn's 'See, Judge, Act', in the US, Catholic Worker, Dorothy Day... During the late 1940s and the 1950s, it became more complicated with the Iron Curtain and anti-Communist militancy.

But, underlying the different stances, there was a common belief in human dignity, human equality, social rights, respect and justice, pay, conditions, right of appeal against authoritarian oppression, the government or, as in this case, union thugs.

Jesus himself, especially in the parables, tells stories of human work, sowers in fields, labourers in vineyards, servants entrusted with money, as well as cautionary stories of bullying, unjust fellow-workers, and the servant being sacked, cooking books to ensure future goodwill from creditors. And he chose working men to be close confidantes, Peter and Andrew, James and John, fishermen.

Father Barry does not appear in a great number of scenes in *On the Waterfront.* He is challenged about his mission by a young woman friend, Edie (Eva Marie Saint), who urges him to work outside the church building. And it is Father Barry who is able to act as conscience-guider for Marlon Brando's Terry Molloy, to take responsibility, make hard decisions no matter what the threat of brutality, whatever the risk.

With all the range of priests on screen, and the wide variety of manifesting Christ-characteristics, Father Barry and his sermon still stand out as a priest Christ-figure.

The Miracle Worker (1962)

Annie Sullivan (and Helen Keller)

THE MIRACLE WORKER who comes most readily to mind is Jesus himself. The Gospels, we might say, are abundantly miraculous. And following in the line of the Old Testament prophets, especially Isaiah, these miracles – the blind seeing, the deaf hearing, the lame walking – are signs that God's reign is at hand. Which would mean that anyone who contributes to such healings, can be seen as another Jesus, a sign of the presence of God in our world.

The play, and then the film, of *The Miracle Worker* (1962) is the story of Annie Sullivan, the site-impaired teacher who undertook the education of Helen Keller, both deaf and blind, not restoring her sight and hearing but enabling her to come alive in her world. The significant life of Helen Keller, her place in American society, her contribution to the betterment of American society, admiration for her throughout the world, are, we might say, signs of God's reign in our world. Annie Sullivan certainly achieved a miracle of raising Helen to new life.

The Gospels have stories of Jesus healing the blind, enabling them to see. And when John the Baptist sends messengers to Jesus to ask if he is truly the one to come, Jesus quotes the prophetic texts. It seems that in the early Christian communities, such stories were told, went their rounds before the texts were written down – several blind men, Bartimaeus (Mark 10, and the drama of the man born blind (John 9).

One of the key elements of Jesus healing is his eliciting from the person requesting a cure a statement of what they wanted. He asks Bartimaeus: 'What would you have me do for you?' And the profoundly simple reply, ' Lord, that I may see'. Jesus does not impose healing. Healing is a response to a request.

In the film, episodes focus on Annie and her work with Helen as a young child. Once you see the film, Annie Sullivan will always be Anne Bancroft, dark glasses, good-mannered, but unabashedly firm, taking her place in the Keller household. And the young Helen Keller will always be Patty Duke, an extraordinarily vigorous performance. The two actresses had performed together on stage and knew how to communicate their struggles, physical struggles, the demands, exasperation and the need for infinite patience for Helen to be able to emerge from her world of silence and darkness. It is Helen's parents who ask for some kind of healing for their daughter – bewildered, dismayed, anxious – as they watch Annie's education of Helen.

And exasperation is a key word. In fact, exasperation is very much a Jesus-word, and therefore a word for a Christ-figure. The disciples and the apostles could be very slow learners. And a frustrated Jesus could bemoan out loud, 'How long have I been with you...'. Even after the resurrection, when Thomas had been absent from Jesus' initial appearance and was fulfilling his claim to be 'Doubting Thomas', Jesus showed great forbearance with him instead of exasperation again, inviting him to touch his wounds. Something like Annie Sullivan's joy as Helen emerged to be the significant woman that she was.

Perhaps an image of Annie and Helen Keller that resembles the Gospels is the culmination of the story of Jesus' encounter with the man born blind. There were bewildered parents. There were supercilious authorities. There were blame games about the blind man and his condition due to something handed on from his parents, their having done some wrong. The blind man doesn't see Jesus in the dramatic encounter. Rather, he follows Jesus' advice, washes his eyes in the pool of Siloam. And it is only later, in an encounter with Jesus quietly in the temple, able to see him, that they are able to have a quiet conversation and Jesus encouraging him. Eventually, Helen will be able to accept Annie and appreciate what she has done for her.

One thing that the film of *The Miracle Worker* does not shy from is the long time that it takes for Annie to communicate with Helen, the long time in Helen's discovery, through moments of touch, the smell and taste of food, but the frustrated tantrums of a child, the moods, physical lashing out – they can be seen if you Google YouTube – powerful scenes as Annie literally fights back, asserts her own strongmindedness, perseveres against the odds, even at table with visitors, trusting that all could be well, all will be well.

Helen Keller went on to be a public figure, living to the full – within her limitations – the life that Annie Sullivan had enabled. It is not difficult to consider Annie Sullivan as a Christ-figure. And her work with Helen, her healing and education, demanding of time and energy, patience and perseverance, is an example of the reign of God in our world.

To Kill a Mockingbird (1962)

Atticus Finch

JESUS DECENT. The decent Jesus.

I don't think I have ever heard Jesus referred to this way. Have you? And yet, this is one of the most basic human qualities. Decency is the quality of those we might call ordinary people, you and I, living our lives as best we can in our particular circumstances. In the past, it might have been called an Everyman quality – and while the intention is important, Everyperson doesn't quite make the grade. It's a challenge to find a helpful right word.

The reason for highlighting Jesus as decent is that a film character who exemplifies this decency is Atticus Finch, immediately recognised by many as the hero of Harper Lee's *To Kill a Mockingbird*, personified on screen by Gregory Peck. The American Film Institute has singled out Atticus Finch as the greatest movie hero of the 20th century. Many comment that Gregory Peck's performance is authentic because he was playing himself (and interestingly, he is buried in the crypt of Our Lady of the Angels Basilica in Los Angeles).

What are some of the words that contribute to our understanding of decency? Personal integrity. Being true to oneself, authenticity. Qualities of courtesy, respect. The decent person does not seek to stand out, but is admired for this integrity and authenticity.

Which raises the question: what Gospel stories showed Jesus as decent? Stories that help us to see qualities that mark a decent Christ-figure? Could we say that initially, as Jesus began his ministry, he was recognised as a decent man? People started to listen to him. They started to follow him. More and more people followed him. His decency was attractive. Then people realised that he was religious, authentically religious. And they grew to realise that he was a truly spiritual man, a man of God.

All the Gospels show how approachable Jesus was. Nobody was afraid of him. Rather, many were eager to approach, to talk, to ask a favour, to be healed. The leper was prepared to break all the social regulations and come close to Jesus to be healed – and Jesus replied, 'Of course, I want to'. The woman gatecrashing Simon's banquet was drawn to him in her regrets for her life. Even Zacchaeus climbed a tree to get a glimpse of Jesus and was glad to welcome him into his house for a meal.

Jesus was concerned about how people were – compassionate when he thought they were like sheep without a shepherd, ready to feed them in their thousands out in the wilderness – and ready to parlay ironic barbs with the Syro-Phoenician woman who wanted her daughter healed. It was the same with the early apostles – Andrew and John wanting to know where he lived and his inviting them to spend the day with him. And Philip taking him to see Nathaniel – and Jesus' welcome to Nathaniel – a fine description of Jesus himself, one translation saying 'a man incapable of deceit'. An older translation says 'a man without guile'.

Which means that we can look at Atticus Finch in the novel and in the film through this perspective of decency. In the state of Alabama, from the early decades of the 20th century, Atticus Finch stands out in terms of justice in his community. He is presented as a loving father, instilling in his daughter, Scout, a sense of doing what is right. In a racist and segregated community, he takes on justice for the oppressed black citizens. He goes to court. He interrogates the witnesses wisely. He demonstrates the innocence of the accused. He is threatened because of his sense of justice, a lynch party, hostile, threatening him as he sits on his porch. The father of the girl who was raped spits in Atticus Finch's face. He believes in fairness – the rain falls on the just and the unjust alike – but justice is for the oppressed: the American principle is 'Justice for all.' And while the jury finds the accused guilty, the men and women in the gallery, the segregated black men and women, stand in the court to applaud him and give him respect for the justice he has sought.

Another venture of the American Film Institute is to nominate 100 of the best quotes from films. They include this one from *To Kill a Mockingbird*:

> You never really understand a person until you consider things from his point of view, until you climb inside of his skin and walk around in it.

When we consider this quote, and any other saying about walking in someone's shoes, we realise that this really is a description of the Incarnation, that God came to earth in Jesus, in his skin, walking around in it, God seeing our experiences and lives through the human eyes of Jesus. God experiencing human decency.

The Sound of Music (1965)

Maria (Maria von Trapp)

A CONFESSION! Second thoughts, even third thoughts and more about whether to include Maria, Maria von Trapp, amongst the Christ-figures. Then wondering why. 'This is one of my favourite films...' is probably the song of millions of fans, from the mid-1960s when *The Sound of Music* won the Oscar for best film, when thousands went to see the film in cinemas and returned and returned (screening in Sydney's Paris Theatre in Liverpool Street from April 1965 to October 1968). And perennially screened on television. On the level of popularity, and not underestimating in any way Julie Andrews' contribution to the popularity, Maria von Trapp was an interesting character.

Perhaps the hesitation was a memory of how the critics, at the time, were not complimentary to the film. Sentimental was one of the immediate responses. I have relied for many years on the reminder that W. Somerset Maugham noted that sentimentality was only sentiment that we did not approve of! There were words like mawkish, mushy (and the reported comment from Christopher Plummer that that was how he found the film – shame! But I gather he repented later!!).

Most of us have enjoyed it, and more than once. So Maria and Maria von Trapp as a Christ-figure.

The heading says both Maria and Maria von Trapp. It is a reminder that she was Maria in herself before she went to the von Trapp family. In those early sequences of the film, the camera circling down on her and the Austrian Alps and the hills alive with the sound of music, she is a young woman of verve, a bringer of joy, charming everyone to be their better selves, and despite 'what do we do with a problem like Maria?', her presence was all for the good in the lives of the nuns.

And, of course, she was a catalyst for good in the von Trapp family, mellowing the militaristic Captain von Trapp (startled as he blew the whistle for the children to introduce themselves – and Maria asking the seemingly innocuous question that shocked him, 'when do they play?'). She was something of a jester. She was joy. And she enlivened each of the children with play, song, the spirit of life. Doh, Ray, me... And lonely goat herds.

And then Maria von Trapp, becoming something of a wisdom-figure for the children and for her husband. A friend told me that a client in counselling trying to describe her relationship with her husband could only fall back on the scene where, across the room and past those who were dancing, the gaze between Maria and the Captain brought to life the fullness of love, even unspoken. Come to think of it, the first time I saw *The Sound of Music* was in Rome, dubbed, even the songs, into Italian (and at this time, as late as 1965, the songs from the nuns were cut from the release – Italian nuns didn't do that kind of thing – which I would vouch for). The point was, seeing the film in an auditorium next to what was then called the Holy Office, with a thousand or so clerics, one could feel early in the film those clerics drawn to her, falling in love, with Julie Andrews/Maria.

And in the war crisis, when the advice of the nuns early in her life was to 'climb every mountain', she and the family literally had to do this, to struggle through the mountains to freedom.

There are many stories told of Maria von Trapp in the years after the war, resuming the pre-war tours and performances of The Trapp Family Singers – in fact, she spent some time during the 1950s working with three of her children with the Missionaries of the Sacred Heart in the Milne Bay Mission of Eastern Papua. And then she moved to the mountains of Vermont, opening The Trapp Family Lodge, its title symbolic, *Cor Unum*. She lived a full and sometimes unexpected life!

Cries and Whispers (1971)

Agnes

AGNES, the Latin, *agnus*, meaning lamb.

Cries and Whispers is one of Ingmar Bergman's most beautiful films to look at, a stately period setting, red rooms, black and white costumes, another world. But with its religious overtones, Bergman suggests that we go back to the biblical aspects of the Lamb. Jesus, of course, is singled out by John the Baptist as the Lamb of God, the Lamb who takes away the sins of the world. This leads us to the *Second Isaiah* from the sixth century BC.

There are two images of the Lamb. The first is in chapter 41, the image of God who tends the chosen people like the lamb that he picks up in his arms for safety, tenderly holding the lamb close to his breast. God is a good and kindly shepherd. However, there is a much grimmer picture of the Lamb in chapters 52–53. This time, the lamb is the sacrificial victim, going silently to being slaughtered, but a death that has meaning, because the lamb dies instead of the people, bearing the sins of the people. This is the image of the Servant of God, from the four songs in *Second Isaiah*, the beloved and chosen one, who is gentle in mission, is consecrated from the womb and commits his cause to God, who listens like a disciple, but is rebuffed, slapped and spat upon, ultimately the Servant who dies for the sake of the people. The Gospels and the letters in the early church see Jesus as this sacrificial lamb, the Lamb of God, the Agnus Dei.

Agnes is at the centre of *Cries and Whispers*. She is a gentle soul, fragile, ill, suffering agonies from cancer, about to die. She is presented as a suffering Christ-figure. But, we might ask, whose sins is she bearing? Those of her two sisters, Maria and Karen. They both come to visit Agnes as she is dying. It is quite clear that both are in need of some redemption. Maria is a self-centred woman, fickle and smug, her mother's favourite growing up, married but unfaithful. Karen, by contrast, is a cold and haughty woman, seemingly unemotional, who has mutilated herself to repel her husband.

With their sister dying, it is an opportunity for Maria and Karen to reflect on their life together as children, their growing up, an opportunity for a kind of examination of conscience for them. And this experience of sharing their sister's dying does have some effect – even if it is seen, both realistically and symbolically, in just their hands touching. They have been touched by the sacrifice of Agnes.

But, Bergman has inherited a severe Christianity, his father a minister in the Church of Sweden (dramatised in his *Fanny and Alexander*), that while redemption comes from the blood of Christ covering our sinfulness, initial redemption may not be permanent redemption. What follows after Agnes's death is a dream apparition. She comes back to the sisters. They are challenged again – and failure of conversion seems inevitable. Jesus has taken away the sins of the world in his death but it does not mean that repentance and redemption always take place.

But, Bergman does show that there is a Christ-figure for Agnes herself. Agnes, in her suffering has not been abandoned. Her Christ-figure is Anna, the family servant. As she lies dying, Agnes is cradled by the buxom Anna as if breastfeeding her. But, after her death, Agnes lies on Anna's lap, a moment of contemplation for the audience to appreciate what has happened, a beautiful Pietà. Later, Anna, treated with mean-mindedness by the sisters, will read in Agnes's diary of a moment in the past, an account of a visit with Maria, Karin and Anna, a shared, nostalgic moment on a swing. Where Agnes wrote that 'come what may, this is happiness'. Redemption is not impossible.

The minister at Agnes's funeral (reminding audiences of the priest struggling with faith in *Winter Light*) prays a Christ-figure prayer:

> If it is so that you have gathered our suffering in your poor body, if it is so that you have borne it with you through death, if it is so that you meet God over there in the other land, if it is so that he turns his face towards you, if it is so that you can speak the language that this God understands, if it is so that you can, then speak to this God, if it is so, pray for us... Pray for us who are left here on the dark, dirty earth under an empty and cruel Heaven. Lay your burden of suffering at God's feet and ask him to pardon us. Ask him to free us at last from our anxiety, our weariness and our deep doubt. Ask him for a meaning to our lives. Agnes, you who have suffered so unimaginably and so long, you must be worthy to plead.

Storm Boy (1976)

Fingerbone

A CHRIST-FIGURE IN Australian culture? A member of the indigenous peoples of the land, an Aborigine?

There have been many historical stories in novels, music, films about the colonial behaviour of the newcomers to the land, of battles, of the massacres, of racist attitudes, a Constitution which did not acknowledge Aboriginal peoples as citizens, with rights, of not acknowledging Aboriginal military service at the front in two world wars, of racism, of condescending mean-mindedness.

Why not an Aboriginal character who personifies great qualities and who, without condescension, could be truly considered as Christ-like? Pre-eminent dancer and actor, political activist, David Gulpilil. Gulpilil has acted in Australian cinema for fifty years. He was introduced as a teenager in *Walkabout*, on his ritual rite of passage, befriending lost school children, helping them to survival and safety, communicating with them without benefit of a common spoken language. But, his most attractive role, to audiences of all ages, adults and children, was as Fingerbone in the 1976 version of *Storm Boy* – a crowd-pleaser in its day and ever since.

Fingerbone is a young man, who has made a mistake and has been exiled from his tribe, has had a variety of work experiences, but still preserves an innate dignity. He is inspired and enlivened by the myths of the Dreaming, creative cultural tales and memories, a way of interpreting life, the bond with the land, the harmony with nature, land and sea, flora and fauna. He is at home despite the difficulties. He belongs. He is intelligent. He also lives with what is called emotional intelligence.

We might like to ponder Christ-resemblances. We might like to consider Jesus in his incarnation as something of an exile from heaven, from his father, no fault at all, but a willingness to share in all our human experiences with us. In his public life, he is a wanderer, traversing the land, the plains of Galilee, the mountains of Samaria, the desert of Judaea, the valley of the Jordan. He tells stories that are laced with images of the land, with nature. He has a heritage, the Jewish Scriptures which inspire him, which he quotes, which he sees himself fulfilling. He has a sense of belonging and self-giving.

Fingerbone comes across a morose father, a fisherman, living isolated in the Coorong of South Australia with his young son, Mike. He befriends Mike. He becomes a mentor for Mike. When we think about Jesus and his disciples, especially the twelve, we realise that Jesus was their friend, they his friends, and he a mentor to them.

A mentor is a catalyst, a catalyst for positive change, for betterment. This is what Jesus did with the twelve – and even Jesus did not have a perfect record with his friends. He had his Judas.

Fingerbone befriends Mike, gains his confidence, Mike being more and more comfortable with Fingerbone, happy in his company. Mike has potential to grow into a young man but, in his isolated situation, with his father's emotional problems, the potential could be crushed. Fingerbone enables Mike to come more alive, to feel the joy of companionship and friendship, to discover, with zest, the beauty and aliveness of nature. Fingerbone urging to learn, even to go to school, for Mike to relate to his father.

But, what we all remember are the birds, the pelicans. Our image of Storm Boy is of him sitting, embracing the large pelican, Mr Percival, content.

Storm Boy, however, is not just a happy story, not a fairytale. Fingerbone has learnt in his exile from his tribe that life can be hard, is hard. And when the shooters arrive (with symbolic memories of shooters of the past arriving with deadly force at Aboriginal settlements), we are reminded that we are also in a dark world, a sometimes sad world. And as Mike's favourite, and our favourite, pelican, Mr Percival is shot and dies, we realise that he is a symbolic reminder of sacrificial deaths.

(There has been a remake of *Storm Boy* in 2019. the adult Mike, remembering his past. It is again the vivid story of Mike, his father, the pelicans, Mr Percival. And there is the pleasure of seeing Gulpilil playing, this time, Fingerbone's Dad.)

Star Wars (1977)

Obi-Wan Kenobi

WHERE IS THAT TEXT in Matthew's Gospel about not calling anyone Master or Rabbi? It is there in chapter 23, Jesus being really fierce in his denunciation of the behaviour of the religious leaders, urging that we do what they say but do not do what they do. He says we are all brothers and sisters and we have one master, the Christ. He can be called a Master and, with Mary Magdalene in the garden at the resurrection, she calls him Rabbi.

Which is a way of introducing a screen Master, and a worldwide acceptance, now for decades, that in a galaxy far, far away, there was a place for a master and mentor, an archetypal sage, admired by everyone. He is that Jedi Master, Obi-Wan Kenobi. Having said that, I feel rather relieved because in recent times I have been getting advice from friends – and they are not as young as they used to be – suggesting that I include *Star Wars* in my *Dear Movies* list and not forget *Star Wars* and Christ-figures. So here we are.

George Lucas said that the role required a certain stability and gravitas for the character, needing a very strong actor to play the part. The choice was Alec Guinness (not exactly an expected science fantasy presence). But Harrison Ford, as Han Solo, said, 'It was, for me, fascinating to watch Alec Guinness. He was always prepared, always professional, always very kind to the other actors. He had a very clear head about how to serve the story'. So, the older Alec Guinness, bearded and veiled, with his resonant, familiar voice, became the exemplar of the Master.

And what is the role of a Master? The Master instructs, guides, accompanies, inspires, serves as a mentor to his followers, disciples. Obi-Wan Kenobi was a mentor to the older generation of Jedi

Knights, including Annakin, and it was to his distress that, even though Annakin was trained in the light, in the power of the Force, evil was more attractive and he chose the Dark Side. (Not every Master had 100% success when one thinks of Judas.) So, Obi-Wan Kenobi had to emerge from his hidden life, from his seclusion as a hermit, in old age, to instruct Annakin's son (and perform the dreaded task of revealing to the son his father's dark side), Luke Skywalker.

With Wars in the title, and continued battles in space, it was inevitable that there would be weapons. (Even Jesus said we had to find weapons to confront and challenge people.) And every boy from 1977 knew what a laser sword was and enjoyed playing, with an equality gender catch up by 2015 when Daisy Ridley's Rey became a knight and 'The Force Awakens'). Obi-Wan Kenobi was also a rescuer, a saviour against the attack of the Black Star, giving his life for his disciples, bequeathing a heritage, Luke discovering that Leia was his twin sister, but living on in spirit, his voice ever-present, inspiring.

(We're bypassing Obi-Wan Kenobi's origin story, Ewan McGregor, in the episode that hasn't quite stayed in the collective memory so affectionately or vividly, *The Phantom Menace*.)

But, of course, we should be considering The Force. In many ways, religious educators were rather pleased that during the 1970s, the possibility of a transcendent power, something of the divine, even of God, could emerge in *Star Wars*. It did lead to a kind of Deism, a general sense of a transcendent presence. It even led to a number of enthusiasts proclaiming Jedi Knights as a religion, even for census purposes. And it had that parallel to the liturgy greeting, 'The Lord be with you'. But, it is not a bad thing to hope that The Force, whatever it be, whatever powers it had, would be with us.

And of course, we might say that in world conversations, 'going over to the Dark Side' means the choice of evil.

But The Force also introduced a wider consideration of the Christian tradition of the Trinity, especially a focus on the Spirit, the Holy Spirit. Obi-Wan Kenobi himself, after his death and continued risen life, was in the spirit, communicating that spirit to Luke. And we remember the language of Jesus, filled with the spirit, promising the spirit, breathing forth on the disciples his spirit, Jesus and inspiration, inspiration having its basic meaning with breath and breathing life. At the beginning of the Jewish Scriptures, the spirit hovers over the void but then creates every aspect of the world.

Of course, this is all symbolic. It is all allegory. There are indications and suggestions, religious elements, evocative elements – and it would be interesting to read a very serious study on the meaning of The Force and how it influenced cultural thinking and religious thinking over the last decades.

Alec Guinness, a devout Catholic convert himself, playing priests in *Father Brown*, *The Prisoner*, *Monsignor Quixote*, impressed younger audiences as a Jedi Master of integrity – and perhaps to more serious audiences, a touch of credibility that Obi-Wan Kenobi could be seen as something of a Christ-figure.

Silkwood (1983)

Karen Silkwood

EACH OF US IS CALLED to be a Christ-figure in our lives. And since most of us live lives out of the headlines, not seeking the limelight, we can look to Christ-figures from what can be called 'ordinary life'. But, for some who live their ordinary lives, situations (or providence) can single them out from more forthright response, upfront activity, some heroism, some headlines.

Which could be a rationale for the choice of Karen Silkwood as a Christ-figure, especially as dramatised in Mike Nichols' 1983 film, *Silkwood*, with yet another versatile and different performance from Meryl Streep. Karen Silkwood grew up in Texas, educated there, married with three children, betrayed by an unfaithful husband, then moved to Oklahoma, was hired as a chemical technician, working at a fuel fabrication plant making plutonium pellets. Life and work on an assembly line. She joined the Oil, Chemical and Atomic Workers Union, was elected to their board and charged with investigating health and safety issues. She gave testimony to the Atomic Energy Commission with a list of alleged breaches of health and safety standards.

And some Christ-figure characteristics?

When we come to think of it, Jesus, before his mission, lived a very ordinary life at Nazareth, no headlines. In fact, he was scoffed at, 'can anything good come out of Nazareth?'. Or, 'surely he is the carpenter's son', not exactly a ringing endorsement. And from the Judaean point of view, his accent was obviously local (provincial!), as the maid said to Peter, hearing him speak, 'surely you are from Galilee'. So, Jesus grew up in trade, manual work, lower class as one might say, few opportunities, limited education with some home schooling, but enough to enable him to converse with the religious leaders when he was lost in Jerusalem as well as to be invited to read the Scriptures in the synagogue 'as he usually did', yet the butt of an amazed question, 'where did he get it all from?'.

However, despite the limitations, Jesus of Nazareth as a character, as a person, emerged full of energy, decisive, taking on responsibilities, acting and speaking with integrity, authenticity, prepared to take risks, altruistic, thwarted, persecuted – and death. Which is something of the pattern of Karen Silkwood, even to death. Suffering high contamination from plutonium, preparing all the documents for the Atomic Energy Commission, she was killed in a mysterious car crash – and younger than Jesus, dying at 28.

The Gospel reference that comes to mind is the parable of the talents, the master going on his travels and giving employees finance (with a handy translation in Gospel texts of 'talents'), entrusting them to use those talents profitably and to give an account of their stewardship. Karen Silkwood found that she had been endowed with more talents than her upbringing and early life might have suggested. And at her untimely death, she could have been praised as 'well done, good and faithful servant'.

There was also the pattern of her challenge to the authorities. She was not a fire and brimstone person. Not that she wasn't exasperated, and that is very clear in the film. Rather, working with within the ethos of the union for the good of others, she investigated, she noted, she spoke out with some authority, with convictions in the hope of helping others. Concerning the powers-that-be, affluent, unscrupulous, uncaring for the good of workers, she was in the vein of the prophets, especially that champion of justice, Amos. And Jesus himself, especially when we listen to his outbursts in Matthew 23, had no hesitation in challenging the stances, the standards, the double standards, of authorities.

Who knows what Karen Silkwood might have achieved even if she had the extra five years to reach the age of Jesus when he died? Her experience of the assembly line and the hardships of fellow-workers meant that she emerged from a group that could be described as sheep without a shepherd. And she moved into leadership with solidarity and compassion.

When we think of it, there is a tradition of social-minded films that show leadership on the factory floor, individuals who did not play in their mission/ministry but who responded to people and to difficult situations. (There could have been a chapter here on *Norma Rae*, 1979, with Sally Field, unions and factories, or that provocative campaigner listening to hardships and problems of pollution and contamination, Julia Roberts as *Erin Brockovich*, 2000, – and worth noting that, at the Oscars, each actress won Best Actress awards for these roles. And their names alone, as with Silkwood, enough to attract audiences.)

Gorillas in the Mist (1988)

Dian Fossey

> Look at the birds in the sky. They do not sow or reap or gather into barns; yet your heavenly Father feeds them... Think of the flowers growing in the field; they never have to work or spin; yet I assure you that not even Solomon in all his regalia was robed like one of these (Matthew 6:26-29).

JESUS WAS NOT an environmentalist as such. But he was vividly aware of his environment, images that he drew on, agriculture and parables, Gospel appreciation of nature. And of course, there was his scriptural heritage, the singling out of the birds, fish, animals in the Genesis creation story – God saw that it was all very good. And there was the arresting relationship between this creation and created men and women, sometimes referred to as 'masters' of creation, better referred to as 'stewards' of creation. And there was the story of Noah, the flood against the humans, the saving of the animals, two by two, and the prospect of their prospering in the new post-deluge world. There were symbols of God's peace and the oracles of the prophets, like the lion lying down with the lamb. And the continued prayer from the Wisdom literature, 'send forth your spirit and renew the face of the earth'.

Which means there are some Gospel Jesus references and qualities when we consider environmentalists, sometimes eco-warriors, whether they are considered as committed or as fanatic.

Which was the case with Dian Fossey, her journey to Africa to observe the gorillas in the mountains of Congo and Rwanda, to preserve them against poachers and predators, respect and wonder for these creatures. And early in *Gorillas in the Mist*, she expresses the statement that she wants to know 'who I am, where I come from'. With the research into animal evolution, the development of primates, Homo Sapiens, her journey is not just scientific but philosophical, even leading to religious and theological quests. High in the mountains, she says that 'this is as close to God as you can get'.

This was the case with Jane Goodall, the British scientist who studied chimpanzees and whose radio interview sparked the writing of this book. In her long life, she has been much more explicit in pursuing religious themes and theological awareness. Dian Fossey, sadly, was killed in Africa, the mystery of her death never finally resolved. There is documentary material about Jane Goodall, but no feature film. There is also documentary material about Dian Fossey's work, but it was she who has the feature film.

Gorillas in the Mist was intended as a tribute to Dian Fossey and her work. It is not a biography. Rather, it is a portrait of the years in the mountains. And it is also described as inspirational. The wonderful cinematography, the invitation to the audience to journey into Africa, be immersed in the landscapes and the beauty, but also in the lives of the people of those African nations, especially in the 1960s and 1970s, uprisings, civil war in the Congo, traditional taboos (and locals considering her a witch), movement towards independence, some graphic moments of this throughout the film.

And there is a challenge to audiences from western cultures. Dian Fossey does have presumptions about being an American, an innate sense of superiority, gung-ho in her U.S. presuppositions which she has to deal with as she works with her generous guide and associate, Sembagare, widening her social horizons.

But the value to an audience embracing environmentalist principles and action, are the many sequences of the gorillas themselves (a blend of actual animals and computer graphics), an opportunity to marvel at the size of the creatures, their way of life, communication, the old and the young, at home in the forests, surviving. In fact, as they live their lives, and have for centuries, the words of Jesus apply to them, they neither sow nor reap yet we can use the language that God cares for them and their appearance can rival Solomon's regalia. Dian Fossey lives with the gorillas, stalking them, learning and noting, more and more at home, close to them, mimicking them, their climbing all over her and being comfortable with her, personalising them with names.

The gorillas and the threat posed by hunters, their possible extinction, is true for so many creatures, large animals like those in Africa or the subcontinent, elephants, rhinos... Down to the smallest of marsupials, beautiful but tiny birds, insects, the prospects that they become extinct species, diminishing the wonder and beauty of the world.

Dian Fossey's work was supported by National Geographic and, her initial resentment that Bob Campbell, the photographer, should intrude into her work was to change as he suggested that photos would reach wider audiences, audiences who are not aware of the issues. And this film had the same impact in its time – and continues to do so.

But, with the invasion of the poachers, Dian Fossey becomes angry, words, confrontations, physical, some memories of Jesus and the whips and the ousting of the moneychangers from the temple. The anger becomes more obsessive, referring to 'my gorillas', somebody rebuking her that it was not her kingdom. She becomes more vindictive and punitive – not Christ-figure qualities.

The following quotation emphasises how an environmentalist can show the characteristics of the Scriptures and of the Gospel Jesus.

> The Bible is not a book of science, and therefore not of ecology. It does, however, sketch a vision of human ecology, and contemporary readers encounter claims about how to value nature. The Bible's vision is simultaneously biocentric, anthropocentric, and theocentric. The Hebrews discovered who they were as they discovered where they were, and their scriptures can be a catalyst in our ecological crisis.
>
> Holmes Ralston, *Interpreters Journal of Bible and Theology*, 50 (1996), pp. 16-26.

Babette's Feast (1988)

Babette

NO DOUBTS ABOUT BABETTE being an eminent Christ-figure. Who else prepared such an image of the Eucharistic banquet and its grace-filled consequences?

One of the advantages of the film version of Karen Blixen's story (writing under the name of Isaak Dinesen) is that it won the Academy Award for Best Foreign Language film of 1988. So, many audiences worldwide have seen it and appreciated it and its luminous message.

Apparently one of those who was moved by it was Jesuit, Jorge Bergoglio, known in more recent times as Pope Francis. When he was elected in 2013, word went round that *Babette's Feast* was one of his favourite films and many of us who wrote on film were asked to speculate why (my request coming from the U.K.'s *Catholic Herald*). We all did our best, looking again at the film, its Eucharistic spirituality.

But, then, Pope Francis has referred to the film a number of times. And has quoted it in one of his most significant Apostolic Exhortations, *Amoris Laetitia/The Joy of Love* (2016).

> The most intense joys in life arise when we are able to elicit joy in others, as a foretaste of heaven. We can think of the lovely scene in the film *Babette's Feast*, when the generous cook receives a grateful hug and praise: 'Ah, how you will delight the angels!' It is a joy and a great consolation to bring delight to others, to see them enjoying themselves. This joy, the fruit of fraternal love, is not that of the vain and self-centred, but of lovers who delight in the good of those whom they love, who give freely to them and thus bear good fruit' (AL, 129).

The reference line from the film: 'In Paradise you will be the great artist God meant you to be. Oh, how you will enchant the angels!'

While the actual Last Supper seems to have been rather an austere occasion (at least as reported) in terms of food and drink, the emphasis on the Gospel narratives being that of the symbolic way of remembering Jesus and his self-giving passion and death as well as his giving the new Law of Love, it is to be seen in the light of the enthusiastic theme of the Jewish Scriptures, the stories of vineyards, the banquet at the fullness of time, the eschatological banquet, wonderful food, wine that cheers the human heart, 'fine strained wines'.

The achievement of *Babette's Feast* is that the transformation of parishioners takes place before our very eyes, hesitant guests, suspicious minds, the concession to merely tasting a drop of wine, the mellowing effect, the enjoyment of the banquet, the smiles, shy greetings, beginning to communicate deeply again with each other, reconciliation and communion. And it is all summed up solemnly in the General's grace and blessing before the meal – mercy and truth have met.

It is probably important to consider the situation of *Babette's Feast* to understand this transformation. It is the 19th century. Babette is French, moving from the Cafe Anglais in Paris where she was a brilliantly creative chef, to the Jutland countryside, keeping house for two elderly sisters. Babette is a behind-the-scenes Martha-figure, not the Martha of our first Gospel encounter with her where she 'worries and frets about many things' but at the feast celebrating Lazarus come to life, a banquet of joy. There is a Christian context, a Lutheran tradition, a minister who has set up his parish church, strict, perhaps a touch of the cult, pious, righteous, abstemious, rather puritanical in its way. (Remembering that comment about Puritans that they feared that somewhere, somehow, someone was happy – or, in the American version, 'having a good time'.) The pastor had moulded his two daughters in his own image, preventing them from marrying, from having love and family, obedient to his interpreting of God's will – or, rather, his whims made sacred. He has died. The sisters have inherited the church and kept it alive. But, the parishioners have grown older, more crotchety, bickering, suspicious. In need of conversion.

Of course, there are visual delights when Babette wins the lottery, takes nothing for herself, goes on a lavish shopping spree, only the best, to prepare a banquet, the feast, that is meant to bring joy to the hearts of all. To that extent, one might say that Babette is also a lavish God-figure. We share Babette's joy, in the kitchen, with the staff and the boy, at the end, sneaking a glass. Complete selflessness, complete self-giving.

It might be useful to remind ourselves of Gospel texts that Jesus is not a Puritan, nor in the 17th Catholic righteous tradition, Jansenist. His critics thought Jesus ought to be more puritanical, calling him a glutton and a wine bibber. Jesus replies (in the *Contemporary English Version*), 'But the Son of Man goes around eating and drinking, and you say, 'That man eats and drinks too much! He is even a friend of tax collectors and sinners'. Yet Wisdom is shown to be right by what it does' (Matthew 11:19).

Somebody remarked jokingly once that Jesus in Luke's Gospel had a dining ministry! He was at home with Martha and Mary. He could accept an invitation from Simon the Pharisee. He could be comfortable with money fraudsters and prostitutes and tell them the story of the Prodigal son. He could go home with Zacchaeus. And he could feed the 5000. Jesus would have been well at home at Babette's feast.

And the final image of the film is also a heavenly anticipation, the result of the Eucharistic experience, some repentance, reconciliation, atonement, and everyone joining hands and, out in the square, dancing joyfully, a dance of life.

(Some comparisons can be made with *Places in the Heart*, a Depression rural drama with Sally Field – and a literal Eucharistic celebration and communion.)

Babette and the angels are delighted.

Awakenings (1990)

Dr Malcolm Sayer

A CHRIST-FIGURE IS someone who awakens awareness, who is a catalyst for personal awakening. So, it is not difficult to see Dr Malcolm Sayer in *Awakenings* as a Christ-figure. He is based on Dr Oliver Sacks, writer and lecturer, and his experience in the 1960s with patients who had experienced the outbreak of encephalitis lethargica from 1917 to 1928 and lived on in a comatose state. He learned about the impact of the drug L-Dopa on patients with Parkinson's Disease. Several of the patients with encephalitis went on L-Dopa treatment and 'awakened', came to life again, revived. It should be added that one of the main impacts of the film is the performance by Robin Williams as Dr Sayer, one of his quiet and controlled performances (like his counsellor in *Good Will Hunting*). If you have a desire to see Robin Williams as an extrovert, exuberant and clowning doctor, see *Patch Adams*!

Dr Sayer, therefore, is the catalyst, Christ-figure for the patients who awaken, especially Leonard, played by Robert De Niro. Jesus said to Nicodemus that redemption, salvation, come from being born again. Nicodemus is baffled. But Jesus tells him that he must be born again in the Spirit, a spiritual rebirth, an adult rebirth. Jesus also said that he came to give life so that everyone would have life to the full. And he told Martha, grieving at the death of her brother, Lazarus, that he was the resurrection and the life. He brought to life the son of the widow of Naim, weeping at her grief, giving the son back to his mother. He raised the daughter of Jairus, the little girl, to new life and making sure that she had something to eat. And eventually, Jesus brought Lazarus out of his tomb and restored him to his sisters, Martha and Mary. (It is a temptation that cannot be resisted in telling the story of the tour guide in the Cathedral in Larnaca, Cyprus, pointing out the tomb of Lazarus who went on mission there – 'and this is where he was buried the second time'.)

The patients in *Awakenings* are born-again as adults, some in middle age, some older. They have the opportunity to continue their lives, to better their lives, to know themselves, their strengths and weaknesses, form relationships, love. But, they know that death is inevitable and they have to be ready for it, again.

Then the patients themselves become Christ-figures for Dr Sayer himself. He is shy, introverted, withdrawn. In his dealings with the patients, in the challenges that Leonard makes, affirmation as well as difficulties, Dr Sayer has to awaken. Lucy, Bert, Rose, Frank, Rob Orlando, Miriam, Sydney, each with their new life, elicit a change in Dr Sayer, bringing him out of himself, out of his self-isolation. And his devoted nurse, Nurse Costello, is a caring, tender Christ-figure who affirms him.

But here is a different suggestion: *Awakenings* should be seen in itself as a Christ-figure. And who is it a Christ-figure for? The audience.

Awakenings is a catalyst for our own awakenings as we watch. In the patients, we see newborn adult life – something which, as we look at ourselves, we must do each day. And this is particularly true if we experience a personal crisis and have to make judgment on ourselves. We have to ask what is the quality of my life? Of our lives? What is it to be a person, what is it to be sentient, emotional, intelligent, free to make decisions. We have to be awake to responsibilities, a sense of responsibility. As viewers of *Awakenings*, we are made more deeply aware of the quality of life, how we are challenged to experience the quality of our lives.

Going back to Jesus of the Gospels and his wanting everyone to have life to the full, the suggestion would be to contemplate aspects of what is called the Last Discourse in John's Gospel, chapters 14-17, the chapters after the Last Supper. Jesus is talking to the disciples now as friends. He praises those who lay down their lives as friends. Thomas asks Jesus for guidance in his friends' lives – and he replies that he is the Way, the Truth and the Life. What is the way and the truth in our reborn lives?

An apt quotation from a commentary: 'At the end of the film, Dr Sayer tells a group of grant donors to the hospital that, although the awakening did not last, another kind – one of learning to appreciate and live life – took place'.

Edward Scissorhands (1990)

Edward

WE USUALLY EXPECT a human character to be considered as a Christ-figure. Here is an exception. *Edward Scissorhands* may not appeal – it will depend on one's sensibilities for fairytales and allegories, symbols or a preference for facts and reality. Edward is not human. He is a puppet come alive.

This film is a contemporary fairy tale, with touches of the Gothic and the magic castle, some moments of Beauty and the Beast, as well as a spoof on modern suburbia and consumerism. The two blend very nicely, fantasy and reality.

The fairytale: in the Castle, high above the town, an elderly inventor is creating a puppet, wanting to bring him alive as the perfect boy. But, he is having difficulty in shaping the hands, substituting scissors until the hands are perfectly formed. But, the inventor sadly dies, the hands incomplete. And Edward, a creation, with a personality to be developed, is stranded alone, until he is welcomed down into the town by the visiting Avon Lady. I hope you are still with it!

Audiences with a religious perspective may will be thinking of God, appreciating the scientist as a God-creating figure. Those with science-fiction perspectives may be thinking of Dr Frankenstein and his attempts to create life – with the risk of creating a destructive monster. But, even back in the 1930s, Boris Karloff's creature had some very tender moments before being hounded by the populace. Some religious points of reference, some comparisons, invitations to our imaginations.

With Christ-figures, they are not generally intended as such by the writers and directors. There is a popular example of no intention by Melissa Matheson who wrote ET as a Peter Pan story but then went to the studio and realised the Christ-symbols from her Catholic background (ET coming to the door of the ambulance, dressed in white but the red of his heart pounding rather sacred! Or his farewell to the children at the end of the film echoing the end of St Matthew's Gospel, 'go... I am with you always').

In a way, we could see Edward coming down into suburbia (its artificial neatness, the rows of suburban homes, the malls, plastic and pastel décor...) as someone coming from on high into our world, what the Incarnation might have looked like if it had happened in the late 20th century American middle class suburbs.

So, Edward as a Christ-figure, highlighting Gospel themes? Up in the Castle, the inventor had actually infused knowledge into Edward, creating a high intelligence, imaginative, poetic, even to details of etiquette. One might say he has human qualities and superhuman qualities. And he is first welcomed into the suburban community, even taken to school as a 'Show and Tell' class for the young boy of the house. He is loved by the daughter, Kim, and despite his fearsome shears, he is able to charm the matrons with his tonsorial skills and the shaping of bushes and hedges, topiary art.

In his own way, quite idiosyncratic, Edward, like Jesus, could be a catalyst for profound change.

But there is envy – Kim's Judas boyfriend, Jim, framing Edward in the context of a robbery to defame him, imprison him – and Jim even betraying Edward with a literal Judas kiss. And fickle people turn against Edward, full of rumours, denigration, persecution, chasing him from the town. In a way he follows the pattern from the Jewish Scriptures of the Suffering Servant, initially beloved and peaceful, turned on and despised, eventually sacrificing himself for the people.

Edward is able to escape back to the castle on the hill with the help of Kim and a deadly struggle with Jim. But, he has returned to his heaven, happy in the Paradise Garden, shaping the bushes and hedges.

And his memory lives on, as Kim, seen as a grandmother, recounts to her eager grandchild the fabled stories of Edward Scissorhands. Just as the Christians did after Jesus' death and resurrection.

Mr Holland's Opus (1955)

Glenn Holland

IT WAS A BIT OF A RISK to choose Mr Holland, Glenn Holland, as a Christ-figure. The issue was music. Glenn Holland was initially reluctant, even resentful, as he began teaching, but then he gradually settled, accepted this vocation, became a long-time music teacher.

And the risk? Gospel references to music.

They are few, very few, and far between. In fact, it is worth Googling 'Jesus and music, Gospel references'. Quite a number of Old Testament references, especially to Psalms, come up. But there was one Gospel reference, Matthew 26:30 when, at the end of the Last Supper, 'after psalms had been sung', Jesus and the apostles went to the garden of Gethsemane. No mention of the singing in Mark, Luke or John.

The prayerful hymns of Zechariah, Mary and Simeon in Luke 1 and 2 are popularly referred to as Canticles.

However, a memory stirred: the older brother of the prodigal son coming back to the house from the farm and hearing music and dancing – not pleased and refusing to go in. And then there is another reference, petulant children not pleased when pipes are played and the other children wouldn't dance. That was Jesus in Luke 7,

> We played the pipes for you,
> and you wouldn't dance;
> we sang dirges,
> and you wouldn't cry.

Jesus was referring to Ezekiel's prophecy in 33:31. 'As far as they (your people) are concerned, you are like a love song beautifully sung to music. They listen to your words, but no one puts them into practice'.

So, Ezekiel the prophet is a song. And Jesús is a beautiful song.

Very few Gospel references to go on if we are to see Glenn Holland as a Christ-figure with reference to music.

But, of course, the point is that he was a teacher. His whole career, even though he resented it at the beginning, not able to travel with his band, wanting to devote himself to composition, his Opus, was a catalyst for his students, to open their horizons, to foster love for music, for composition and performance. Googling did reveal this quote from Martin Luther, 'Beautiful music is the art of the prophets that can calm the agitations of the soul; it is one of the most magnificent and delightful presents God has given us.'

So, *Mr Holland's Opus* offers an opportunity for noting the importance of Jesus as a teacher, and educator, leading students and disciples from their ordinary ways of thinking and acting to broader perspectives, extraordinary perspectives.

When we think of Jesus as teacher, and that phrase occurs so often in the Gospels, 'Jesus taught them...', he explained, he instructed, he took his disciples aside for, we might say, tutorials; he opened eyes, directed them to new horizons. You may be thinking of John Keating, Robin Williams dazzling performance as the rebel-creative teacher of *Dead Poets Society*. John Keating dealt with words, poetic imagination and expression, and he did get his students to stand on their desks to get a different perspective for their learning. He was an enthusiastic and creative idealist, urging his students to Seize the Day, Carpe Diem. Here we have a more and more genial Richard Dreyfuss, notes and melodies rather than poetic words.

No Christ-figure is perfect. In fact, Glenn Holland has some severe limitations. He was able to break through his disappointment and embrace his teaching career, persevering, then blossoming, for many decades. But, this was to the neglect of his family, his not bonding with his son, his son deaf, unable to hear the music. Yet, there was a blessing in Glenn Holland's life, breakthrough communication with his son, his son alerting his father to this absence in his life, and reconciliation.

So Glenn Holland's Opus was not his longed-for musical composition but rather bringing his students to new levels of life, (and of course, they being Christ-figures, each in their own way, to transforming Glenn Holland). And he delighted in their achievements, the young woman who became a governor, and saddened by the young man who died in battle in Vietnam...

Which is a reminder of the theme – so well promoted by Henry Nouwens – that to be an authentic and effective Christ-figure who heals, we all must be 'wounded healers'.

It is commonplace to say that we can be healed by listening to music and that is one of the charms of this film, music in the classroom, awkward student performances, talented student performances, music that encourages, sparks the imagination, gives joy – and elicits experiences which we might call mystical. And the reminder, sad, of Glenn Holland's son, his inability to hear – the classic reminder that Beethoven himself was deaf.

There are many other films with music teachers, teachers of instrumental performance, of choirs, Meryl Streep in *Music of the Heart*, Dustin Hoffman in *Boychoir*, but many of us will go back to our school days, learning to play the piano or the violin or being a member of the school choir, experiences that may have had their difficulties at the time, but were ultimately enriching.

Dead Man Walking (1995)

Sister Helen Prejean

NO QUIBBLE ABOUT nominating *Dead Man Walking* as a Christ-figure film. Sister Helen Prejean seemed an obvious choice in the 1990s. And she still is.

Back in the 1990s, some of us were wondering whether there would be films focusing on religious sisters and their ministry. Numbers joining congregations were lessening. Many sisters in active ministry no longer wore religious habits, but had crosses or religious emblems. No worries about a continuity of films featuring priests. What about the sisters? And then came *Dead Man Walking*, and the world getting to know Sister Helen, seeing her as a young novice making profession in the 1950s, solemn ceremonies, the habit... But then, the 1970s and 1980s, prison chaplaincy and its possibilities, her advocacy of the abolition of the death penalty, stances she has been promoting ever since, more than a quarter of a century since the release of the film. And it was a pleasure to see her sitting beside Susan Sarandon on Oscar night as she received the Best Actress Academy award and the actress acknowledging her.

The first and immediate consideration is that as soon as Caiaphas condemns Jesus, Jesus is a dead man walking.

Before those final steps to the gallows on Calvary, he was scourged, crowned with thorns, mocked, defeated in popular choice by Barabbas, crowds yelling for his death. And literally, on the road, there he was, shouldering the cross, dead man walking. No chaplains. Although he did experience some comfort and consolation – the Catholic imagination in the Stations of the Cross suggesting he met his mother along the way, his bleeding face wiped by Veronica. There were the weeping women of Jerusalem. And Simon of Cyrene helping Jesus to carry his cross. Even on Calvary, the 'good thief' prayed to Jesus. And there was his mother, Mary, the beloved disciple, Mary Magdalene and the women. Jesus did not experience earthly death alone.

The main text that springs to mind from the Gospels about prison ministry is the dramatic scene where the king assembles the sheep and the goats for judgment (Matthew 25) and asks the questions of what they have done or not done, visiting prisoners or not and the revelation that when they did their good deeds, it was for the least of their brothers and sisters, in fact, they did it for Jesus himself. No problem applying that to Helen Prejean. And when we think about the crimes of the man she visited, Matthew Poncelet, he could certainly be described as 'the least of these'. And Sean Penn's performance reveals the many facets of his character, from callous to contrite ('I've never been called a child of God before.').

An ideological Catholic aside: one of the topical aspects of *Dead Man Walking* is the role of ministry and church authorities. Fortunately, when Helen and her sisters picket the prison at the time of executions, campaigning against capital punishment, the bishop is sympathetic. However, the clash is with the official prison chaplain, the priest whose strong belief in the clerical code makes it difficult for him to support a nun sharing in his official appointment. Some obvious Christ-figure comparisons there – not to clerical advantage.

What the film does is to show, in close-up, how prison chaplaincy can work day by day. Sister Helen's role is one of accompaniment, being present with the prisoner, allowing for time, enabling the prisoner to share, to become more aware of what has happened, his responsibility, his guilt. She is not judging him but encouraging him to be able to judge himself. She is not urging him to confess but, rather, to acknowledge what he has done. And in changing times in the Catholic Church, it raises the question of who should absolve sacramentally. Is this limited to the priest? Can it be the role of a prison chaplain?

But, there is a moment of deep shock for Sister Helen – and for the audience sharing her approach to her work. So, involved is she with Matthew Poncelet that she has been insensitive to the feelings of the parents and relatives of the murder victims. They turn on her, and on us as we watch, revealing pain and anguish that she has overlooked. And this is a revelation to her and to us that prison chaplaincy is not simply for the person incarcerated. There are other dimensions. There are others involved, consequences of the crimes. And this continues as a challenge for her throughout the film, even as they sit near each other in the execution witness room.

There are two endings for *Dead Man Walking*.

The first is Matthew Poncelet's dead man walking to his execution. And Sister Helen has to accompany him as he walks. There is a moving moment, especially for those familiar with the St Louis Jesuits' hymn by Bob Dufford, Be Not Afraid... when she sings it quietly. And in his death, she offers a quietly a gentle smile of consolation. 'The last thing to see is the face of love. I will be the face of love for you.'

> Be not afraid
> I go before you always
> Come, follow me and I will give you rest

There is a second ending. And this focuses on the parents of the victims who have felt anger against Sister Helen. We see the Chapel, the camera circling it from outside, and inside is Helen and one of the fathers, so previously hostile, kneeling in prayer, hope of reconciliation and forgiveness. Keys to prison chaplain ministry.

Amazing Grace (2006)

William Wilberforce

NO QUESTION ABOUT William Wilberforce as a Christ-figure, well-known for his fight for the abolition of slavery. And he was a professing Christian to boot – not, perhaps, a particularly apt expression to note his qualities, although he had quite some opposition, social and political, in his time. In his mid-20s, he supported the evangelical wing of the Anglican Church – and in his 30s published a book that he had been working on for some time, *A Practical View of the Prevailing Religious System of Professed Christians, in the Middle and Higher Classes in this Country, Contrasted with Real Christianity*, an exposition of New Testament doctrine and teachings and a call for a revival of Christianity, as a response to the moral decline of the nation (from his *Wikipedia* entry, well worth consulting for the details of his life and career).

(It should be noted, especially as we read the *Wikipedia* portrait, that, while Wilberforce was a champion for the abolition of slavery, he was very conservative/traditional in other views as, say, the place of women in society; and he voted against Catholic Emancipation.)

Amazing Grace is one of those highly enjoyable British heritage-style histories, a portrait of Wilberforce (born 1769), played by Ioan Grufudd as a committed social reformer – supported for many years by his friend, Barbara Spooner, whom he eventually married. The film reminds us that, as a child, he visited John Newton. He is that John Newton, of course, the former sea captain involved so heavily on the slave trade for many years, reformed, repentant, writing what must be the most popular hymn in the English language, *Amazing Grace*, tracing his conversion, the conversion from slave-oppression that Wilberforce was urging on the British public, British society and politics, cities that had profited, prosperity from the slave trade.

> Amazing grace, how sweet the sound
> That saved a wretch like me
> I once was lost, but now am found
> Was blind but now I see.

The film has a telling sequence when Wilberforce goes to visit the elderly John Newton (played by Albert Finney) who is glimpsed mopping a church, dressed in sackcloth. Sackcloth, the biblical garment of repentance.

Wilberforce's gospel themes were twofold. There was the compassion of Jesus in his judgment parable in Matthew 25, the challenge to loving outreach to the sick, the poor, those in prison, freedom for slaves. And there was the continued challenge of the demanding Jesus, repentance and conversion – the Amazing Grace.

> Was grace that taught my heart to fear
> And grace, my fears relieved
> How precious did that grace appear
> The hour I first believed

While there are many sequences in the film dramatising Wilberforce's social and spiritual journey, with the tolls that it made on his health, it is the sequences in the parliament that are well worth considering in terms of Wilberforce as a Christ-figure. He has no trouble in defying the authorities, the double standards, as indicated by his book (which, it is said, was a bestseller in its day and translated into several languages). There are sequences showing some of the horrors of the slave ships and the sometimes frantic meetings conducted by Wilberforce and his group. Some of the most compelling parliamentary sequences highlight the heat of debate illustrating the self-interest and lack of compassion of so many members, indebted to slavers and businessmen. Wilberforce was a political crusader against inhumanity and injustice, not just the promoter of a cause. While his speeches were couched for his fellow-politicians, making demands on their consciences, they can be seen as the Gospel translated into the impassioned rhetoric of political conviction.

> Through many dangers, toils and snares
> We have already come
> T'was Grace that brought us safe thus far
> And Grace will lead us home

The film was released worldwide in February 2007, anticipating the 200th anniversary on 25 March 1807 of the Act for the Abolition of the Slave Trade, banning trading in enslaved people the British Empire. However, it was not until 1833 that the House of Lords passed the bill of abolition – a month after Wilberforce's death.

> And grace will lead us home.

The Courageous Heart of Irena Sendler (2009)

Irena Sendler

On 19 October 1965, Yad Vashem recognised Irena Sendler as Righteous Among the Nations. The tree planted in her honour stands at the entrance to the Avenue of the Righteous Among the Nations. Irena Sendler (1910–2008)

WHO WAS IRENA SENDLER? She was a young woman in Warsaw at the outbreak of World War II. She worked for the city council. When the ghetto was established, she was able to enter in and out, befriending many of the Jewish families, helping with food and with other support. She formed a band of co-workers amongst the Poles – Catholic Poles – some of whom did not want to join but others who were prepared to give their lives.

Ultimately, she was able to smuggle out babies and children from the ghetto and place them in foster families during the war and in some convents. She was helped by the local parish priest. 'From October 1943 she was head of the children's section of Zegota, the Polish Council to Aid Jews. Zegota planned their strategies and devised routes to smuggle the children, some in boxes hidden under bricks on wheelbarrows, others through sewer systems, and still others brazenly escorted through the front door of the city hall hand-in-hand with their saviours'. (I would recommend further Googling and *Wikipedia* searches on Irena Sendler and Zegota.)

When we think of films that have brought world attention to the saving of Jews during the war, we immediately think of

Oscar Schindler (Thomas, Kenneally/Ark, Steven Spielberg/List), *Schindler's List* (Oscar for Best Picture of 1993). He was high profile, industrialist, something of a playboy, but rose to the occasion of saving his workers. Irena Sandler had a more modest profile. A one-hour documentary film was made after her death, In the *Name of Their Mothers*. Our focus here is a feature film, made for television, *The Courageous Heart of Irena Sandler*, 2009, with Anna Paquin as Irena. with Irina Sandler herself appearing at the end of the film. It is said that she saved 2500 children.

All those who saved persecuted Jewish adults and children can be seen as Christ-figures. Irina was not alone in her work. She relied on her Jewish friend, Stefan. There also the local priest. There were her co-workers, sometimes dressing as nurses, doctors and their support, anonymous shopkeepers evading Nazi inquiries, drivers of the vehicles.

'I was in prison and you visited me' (Matthew 25:36) – or, rather, 'I was in prison and not only did you visit me, you found ways to rescue me, to free me, to venture into and hide in labyrinths of hit and miss in disguise, to find friends and shelter, some peace until the persecution was over'. Jesus did not say this exactly but he might have said it in reference to the range of extraordinary efforts during World War II in saving Jewish children, Jewish workers, destined for the concentration camps and volunteers, some high profile, some ordinary family people who dared to shield and save the Jews.

At the Last Supper, Jesus gave his New Covenant bequest, his Law of Love, 'Love one another as I have loved you'. And further, 'no greater love is there than to lay down one's life for one's friend' – with the reality of laying down one's day-by-day life for others. This story of Irena Sendler shows how she laid down her life for the children, but then arrested, interrogated, tortured, feet beaten, the women taken out and lined up against the wall to be shot, prepared to die – but a guard helping her, urging her to escape.

With the Polish setting, a Catholic country, strong Catholic tradition, the film is also a challenge to anti-Semitism. The challenge of how devout Catholics over the centuries had absorbed anti-Semitic stances, became persecutors. I recently heard a comment that someone has said his parents were devout Catholics. And then he added, 'but, even better, they were real Christians'. This film is a challenge to our understanding of what real Christians are, seeing real Christians in action.

Another feature of the film is the emotional conflict coming from the apprehensiveness of the Jews about the Polish families, the possibilities of conversion. Irena kept lists and information about the rescued children for families to recover their children after the war. And a postscript with the emotional difficulties for the foster parents, their attachment to the children and surrendering them to their original families.

Questions and challenges – lest we forget.

Invictus (2009)

Nelson Mandela

INVICTUS, INVINCIBLE, UNCONQUERABLE. An apt title for a film about Nelson Mandela. He liked to recite the poem by William Ernest Henley from 1875, especially the final lines, captain of my soul, master of my fate.

> Out of the night that covers me,
> Black as the Pit from pole to pole,
> I thank whatever gods may be
> For my unconquerable soul.
>
> In the fell clutch of circumstances
> I have not winced or cried aloud.
> Under the bludgeonings of chance
> My head is bloody but unbowed.
>
> Beyond this place of wrath and tears
> Looms but the Horror of the shade,
> And yet the menace of the years
> Finds and shall find me unafraid.
>
> It matters not how strait the gate,
> How charged with punishments the scroll,
> > I am the master of my fate:
> > I am the captain of my soul.

Nelson Mandela has been described as a born leader, an authoritative yet empathetic uniter who preached forgiveness and looked for common ground when elected president of South Africa. Many saw his qualities as paralleling the mind and actions of Jesus in the Gospels.

There have been many films about Nelson Mandela, including a film of his own book, *The Long Road To Freedom* (with Dennis Haysbert as Mandela). There is a great deal of footage online to be found by searching on YouTube. However, a way of focusing on the man himself and his work of uniting, is Clint Eastwood's 2009 film, *Invictus*. It dramatises a symbolic event, the Rugby Grand Final of 1995, the membership of the team, the breakthrough with having black players and white players together, Mandela himself putting on the Springbok jersey, and the happy Providence that the Springboks did win.

Invictus has the advantage of Morgan Freeman playing Mandela – and it is said that Mandela himself wanted Freeman to play him.

In thinking about the film and its sports theme, it seemed a good idea to Google Jesus and sport. No entries! As regards the Jewish Scriptures, there was a note about Abraham running to welcome guests. And there was the celebrated sequence of Jacob wrestling with God. In fact, the main sport references come in the New Testament, the Pauline writings, mainly about running races and finishing courses, references in 1 Corinthians, Philippians and the Letter to the Hebrews (12:1). No ready references for *Invictus* and Christ-figures.

Time is rapidly passing and it is over three decades since Nelson Mandela's release from his twenty-seven years imprisonment on Robben island. Which means that teenagers at the time are now in their 40s. What of the memories of, the regard for, Mandela in contemporary South Africa?

And you may have memories of Mandela and South Africa. In 1996, I was amazed that I was able to have a meal in a restaurant in Brakpan, outside Johannesburg, together with an Irish priest and a black African priest who was to leave for Europe the next day for further studies. With what we had heard of life in apartheid times, sitting quietly, normally, in the restaurant within years of Mandela's release and his becoming president, showed that the impossible was possible. And later visits to Robben island, the skyline of Cape Town so near and yet so far, guards who were prisoners at the time showing us around, helping us to imagine what those twenty-seven years of imprisonment, isolation, grinding humiliation and work must have been like.

So, there is great exhilaration in watching *Invictus*. Perhaps a more useful approach to Christ-figure characteristics for Mandela is to focus on his breaking through apartheid, the work of uniting a racially divided country, truth and reconciliation, forging a nation.

I would like to suggest a scene in Zeffirelli's *Jesus of Nazareth*, a favourite sequence, where Jesus is invited to a meal with the tax collectors and prostitutes, as found in Luke 15:1-3, but this time a meal hosted by Matthew. Peter, hostile to Matthew because of his tax collecting demands, refuses to go in. Robert Powell has Jesus speaking the parable beautifully. Peter outside listening, the older brother refusing to go into the prodigal's feast – but able to come in to the meal at the end and be reconciled with Matthew. Something of this happened in South Africa in the 1990s.

And what of Jesus encountering 'foreigners' 'the enemy', at home with them, to others' scandal? The Samaritan woman at the well? The Syro-Phoenician woman taunting Jesus to heal her daughter? And what about the image of the Good Samaritan himself, no hostile barriers, saving the battered traveller, Jesus and the lawyer's seemingly petulant question about 'who is my neighbour?'. And Jesus' blunt, commanding answer, 'go and do the same yourself'?

A way of looking at what Nelson Mandela did with the Springboks is to see it in the light of what could be called 'prophetic symbolic actions'. The prophets of the Jewish Scriptures certainly spoke oracles but they also communicated God's word by their actions – the statement of Isaiah in the temple and his tongue being seared and cauterised by the sacred coals to prepare him for his preaching, or Ezekiel putting on refugees' clothes and exiting Jerusalem by a hole in the wall...

It seems a master stroke of politics and humanity (as Mandela notes several times) to bring black and white people together supporting the national rugby union team when South Africa is hosting the rugby world cup in 1995. The sequences where the meeting of football supporters vote to eliminate the colours and the name of the Springboks and Mandela himself comes to tell them not to because it is depriving the Afrikaaners of something they value (which they had done to the blacks) but to use that for uniting people. Which indicates his shrewdness and vision. The sequence where he persuades his black security officer to accept former white police, from Special Branch, into the bodyguard squad is similarly powerful. Mandela shows his indefatigably driven work ethic.

The training sequences, hard training, making sure the team was fit, then Mandela's order that they should go and coach the black children in the townships, the bus ride, the fears, the shock of some of the men at seeing the townships and the way of life, the boys playing football, the training, the bonds between the team and the kids, black representatives. We see Mandela at work, the television showing the team and the coaching, everybody watching, Mandela valuing the image, a coup for public relations.

The climax, the final match against New Zealand's All Blacks is presented in all its rough and tumble ('soccer is a gentlemen's game played by hooligans and rugby is a hooligans game played by gentlemen').

A prophetic symbolic action – and a promise for hoped-for reconciliation and unity.

The Hunger Games (2012)

Katniss Everdeen

KATNISS EVERDENE? She is 16, a teenager, a girl, part of an oppressed and exploited family, a hunter for food in the forests, intelligent, self-aware, strong, direct, even blunt, in the way she speaks and communicates. A Christ-figure?

The 21st-century has seen the emergence of heroes and superheroes, some from the comic book and graphic novel universe, some from young adult literature, like The Hunger Games series. They are created for younger audiences, the treatment geared towards them and their sensibilities. And their imaginations are stirred by heroes and superheroes – one hopes, as well, that this could steer them towards an alertness and admiration for Jesus' story, with the hero of the Gospels. (And the popularity of these stories and heroes continues as time passes – and youngsters who enjoyed and identified with *The Hunger Games* in 2012 are now in their 20s.)

One of the distinctive features of this kind of storytelling is that it is set in a dystopian world, a post-apocalyptic world, mirroring our own present in some way (and wondering what a post-covid apocalyptic world might be like), but showing destruction, survival and struggle, the emergence of authoritarian dictatorship, brutality and the blunting of sensibilities – and the need for a heroic figure who will stand for good against evil. We might remember that Jesus himself, in his own storytelling, drew on some of the apocalyptic imagination (post-apocalyptic imagination) of the Jewish Scriptures – Armageddon, for instance, from the prophet Ezekiel. Jesus describes times of tribulation, images of tempestuous weather, atmospheres of uncertain dread as one is taken, one left, false prophets, rumours of wars, family members betraying family members, times of dread and the need for faith, for hope, for fidelity. Katniss certainly fulfils these demands. With reference to the Jewish Scriptures, we might remember times of human sacrifice – Isaac saved from death, the era of the judges, the sacrifice of Jethro's daughter... And there were the warrior women, Jael, Esther and Judith.

With the title, *The Hunger Games*, the visuals of the affluent oppressive class (where ideals have been lost, greed substituted), take us back to the Roman Empire, the gladiatorial combats to the death, the fickle crowd, fans at one moment, thumbs down callous condemnations the next. (We see them as completely fickle, crowds who would have cried out in demand for the release of Barabbas if they were goaded.) But this is the future, and everything is televised, the equivalent of statewide brutal Reality TV, the profligate audience caked in an excess of make-up, exaggerated fashion, touch of the ludicrous, determined to be seen. (And a reminder to us that Jesus grew up in a province of this Roman Empire, Pontius Pilate with his Roman traditions, the military...)

The irony of the setting up of *The Hunger Games* is that the contestants are all young, victims of a lottery in their district to choose them, and the use of the euphemism 'tribute'. The younger sister of Katniss is chosen, but Katniss, prefiguring the kindness and self-sacrifice that we shall see during her combats in the games, offers herself instead of her sister. In the process of preparation for the games, with the sympathetic trainer, with the fussy, frivolous fashion designer, supporting her friend from home who loves her, Peeta, she makes friends, ultimately some disciples. She is a person who can command loyalty. And she is not too afraid to defy the authorities, the mini-bureaucrats, the autocratic and murderous President himself, President Snow. And during the games, in the fights for survival, she experiences betrayers.

Katniss is both prepared to fight, which she does, and prepared to die. But, she does triumph, using her wits but no vengeance, not killing her main rival, as was expected, Peeta, but joining with him and both honoured as winners. A kind of resurrection image. But, as President Snow, in his mood, mounts the staircase, we know that there is more and that in the sequels, Katniss will have to show leadership, encourage rebels, be prepared to risk and give her life.

This reflection on Katness Everdeen as a Christ-figure is not particularly subtle. Subtlety is not a quality that stands out in young adult literature and films – rather, there is a direct appeal to the audience, to the younger audience, to their developing sensibilities (subtlety continuing to develop), a growing recognition of heroic qualities and a sense of admiration and inspiration.

Selma (2014)

Martin Luther King Jr

'OUR LIVES ARE not fully lived unless we are willing to die for those we love and what we believe.' One of the many significant quotations from Martin Luther King. Speaking at the award of his Nobel Peace Prize, he said 'the illusion of supremacy has destroyed the truth of equality'. And at the 1963 Washington March, he spoke of the dream of the equality of all.

In the more than half century since his assassination, 'willing to die for those we love and what we believe', 1968, his status has grown as an American hero, even having a holiday named after him so that all continue to remember him (first celebrated in 1986, under two decades after his killing).

The film, *Selma*, was released for the 50th anniversary of the March in Selma, the courage of the marchers on the bridge, set upon by the police, marching again, Martin Luther King kneeling on the bridge before the massed police barrier, his turning the marchers around, roundly criticised, but finding his answer in his prayer – the hearings before the court vindicating him – and interfaith, ecumenical, all races joining together in the celebration of the March on Montgomery.

In 2001, an HBO film, *Boycott*, dramatised the work of Martin Luther King and his associates in Montgomery, Alabama, 1955 and 1956, on the occasion of Rosa Parks not giving her seat to a white passenger and the black community peacefully boycotting the buses, leading to a challenge to the authorities, changes in legislation, further paving the way to the Civil Rights movement in the 1960s.Recommended.

King was seen as a Christ-figure in his time, pastor, along with his father, at the Ebenezer Baptist Church in Atlanta, Georgia. He is seen at prayer. He tries to make decisions based on prayerful discernment. His stances are based on Gospel teachings.

Martin Luther King was not perfect. J. Edgar Hoover and the FBI kept him under constant surveillance, keeping records of his movements, trying to expose him as a 'political and moral degenerate' because of sexual liaisons. We can be reminded of John 8, the story of the woman taken in adultery. The authorities had Jesus under surveillance, wanted to trap him, get him to contradict the law of Moses. King, under surveillance to be trapped, was considered an adulterer – but Jesus had the answer for the woman, and, therefore, for King: forgiven, go and sin no more.

Selma shows us the relationship in his 15 year marriage to Coretta, the strains on the marriage, dangers for their children, her continued support of him – and her campaigning to have the public holiday.

The film offers three steps that King used to raise white consciousness: negotiate, demonstrate, resist. We can see this pattern in the life and ministry of Jesus himself. Jesus was a teacher, an educator, discussing with the religious leaders, his manifesto for negotiation, so to speak, in the Sermon on the Mount. However, as he was spied on, criticised, challenged, he began to demonstrate, as we remember his fiercely rhetorical denunciations of the hypocritical leaders, 'woe to you...' In Matthew 23. Jesus did not back down. He stood by his convictions, resisting the threats of the authorities until they arrested him, tried him, killed him.

Martin Luther King came to believe that he should create fire on the earth and was eager that it should be started. Words of Jesus in his preaching of the reign of God on earth, a message of repentance, change of heart, justice for all eager for that fire of conversion to be lit. And Jesus, so often frustrated in his mission, wept over Jerusalem and the fact that the people would not listen. Martin Luther King, faced with racist bigotry, attitudes which demeaned the black races, the history of slavery, poverty, lynchings, 'there are no words – but God was the first to cry'.

Martin Luther King's words in Washington have been played so often that not only can we see him uttering them but we hear the resonance in his words, 'I have a dream...'.

Much has improved since those words but, sadly, challengingly, they still need to be said and heard. Pope Francis offered a powerful quote in his *Amoris Laetitia/The Joy of Love* (no. 188) from Martin Luther King Jr., whom the pope describes as meeting 'every kind of trial and tribulation with fraternal love'.

Hacksaw Ridge (2016)

Desmond Doss

THE GOSPEL STANCES of Jesus, especially his revoking of 'an eye for an eye' vengeance, would qualify consideration of him as a pacifist. Yes, he did say that he has come to create conflict on the earth, rifts in families, upheaval, denunciations... But it is not exactly Jesus creating this violence. Rather, Jesus knew that discipleship, following him, would be the cause of family dissension, disruption.

Of course, Jesus inherited the theology of the Jewish Scriptures, was grounded in them, read from the texts in the synagogue at Nazareth, was able to reference them in his preaching. He had inherited a language and imagination of God (who, in the Old Covenant at Sinai, was characterised as just, loving and kind, merciful) who was angry, demanding of those who offended him, struck down enemies with vengeance. But with the New Covenant charter of love one another as I have loved you, of laying down one's life, day by day as well as in death, not revoking the Ten Commandments but interpreting them in the light of the Beatitudes, Jesus ultimately was a preacher of peace. Not an eye for an eye but, turn the other cheek. Blessed are the peacemakers.

In world history, pacifists have been seen to be acceptable enough, in theory and in peacetime. When they become conscientious objectors in times of war, public opinion turns against them, even imprisoning them. Yet, there are many stories of such conscientious objectors and their fulfilling different service even in the middle of battles.

Mel Gibson's 2016 *Hacksaw Ridge* provides a fine example of a heroic conscientious objector, pacifist. (Interesting to remember that Mel Gibson, not always a man of peace, even in religious and ethnic controversies, won his Oscar as the warrior, *Braveheart*.) This conscientious objector, Desmond Doss, is described succinctly by *Wikipedia* in an entry about the 2004 documentary about him, *The Conscientious Objector*, an objector who received a Medal of Honor for his service in World War II. Because of his religious convictions as a Seventh-Day Adventist, he refused to carry a weapon. He initially faced opposition, persecution, and ridicule from his fellow soldiers but ultimately won their admiration by demonstrating courage and saving lives as a combat medic'. He was influenced by his mother: no work on the sabbath, vegetarian lifestyle, supporting his family by factory work during the Depression.

This is all dramatised in *Hacksaw Ridge*, with a very sympathetic performance from Andrew Garfield as Desmond Doss, alarmed when young in a struggle with his brother, violence from his father, interpreting the Gospels literally. He acknowledged the reality of World War II, enlisting, not carrying a weapon, mocked in training, but in powerful cinema images of the reality of battles, re-enactments in Okinawa, Desmond Doss is the incarnation of pacifism in the middle of war. And he suffered his own passion, at the age of 25, suffering a left arm fracture from a sniper's bullet while being carried back to Allied lines and at one point had seventeen pieces of shrapnel embedded in his body after a failed attempt at kicking a grenade away from him and his men. (Just as Jesus could be seen as the incarnation of peace in a violent world that ultimately took its toll on him.)

Desmond Doss's story is one of heroism, the saving of seventy-five men, caught in ambush, wounded, his being able to lower them down the cliff face to medical help, saving them from death. And, in the vein of Jesus, wounded himself, ready to die, but he is saved, comes to life again, his resurrection, and honoured by troops and government alike, yet his being modest and retiring.

There are many sequences in *Hacksaw Ridge* – when Desmond Doss is young, during the harshness of his training, in his pacifist activities in the middle of action – that remind us of Jesus pacifist. We can revisit the anguish in the Garden of Gethsemane, Jesus, fearful, even to sweating blood, yet saying yes to what the father has asked of him. He tells Peter to put up his sword when the soldiers arrive. Those who live by the sword, die by the sword (Matthew 26:52). He goes quietly, even willingly, to trial before Annas and Caiaphas, and an enquiring rebuke asking why he has been spat upon, offering the vision of the Son of Man in Daniel 7, coming into the presence of God, not as a defence, but as a declaration of who he was. He is scourged. He is crowned with thorns. He is mocked as a king. And a dismayed Pontius Pilate is shocked, 'Ecce Homo, Behold the Man'. On the cross, Jesus comforts his mother and the beloved disciple, promises joy to the thief crucified with him, begs God's forgiveness on those who have killed him.

There is profound reality in Jesus pacifist – so well imaged in Desmond Doss.

On the Basis of Sex (2018)

Ruth Bader Ginsburg

OBSERVERS AND COMMENTATORS with some familiarity with the Gospels, with Jesus of the Gospels, whether they are believers or not, make remarks that a particular person, especially in some facet of their behaviour, is 'Christ-like'. Such comments have been made about Mahatma Gandhi, about the Buddha, about St Francis of Assisi... So it is not inappropriate to consider American Justice of the Supreme Court, Ruth Bader Ginsburg, a secular Jew, and her work for American law and justice over many decades as a Christ-figure without disrespect to her background and beliefs.

In fact, she had a plaque in her office, a text from the book of Deuteronomy about justice: 'Justice, justice you shall pursue' (Deuteronomy 16:20).

For those wanting background for Ruth Bader Ginsburg, there are two films – a strong documentary featuring many of her speeches as well as very personal sequences, *RBG*, and a feature film dramatising her early years and struggles, *On the Basis of Sex*. That was a quotation from American legislation, RBG preferring 'on the basis of gender'. In fact, part of her Christ-figure characteristics was the care for women, suggesting that men had put them on a pedestal but actually trapped them in a cage. Her comment on her fellow male Justices was to ask them to take their feet off the necks of women.

Perhaps a way of considering Ruth Bader Ginsburg and her commitment to law and justice is to consider her in the tradition of the Jewish Scriptures through those keywords, the Law Charter of the Gospels, the Beatitudes. The first is an affirmation of the 'poor in spirit', taking up the theme of 'the humble of the earth', those who need support. But Ruth Bader Ginsburg also saw the law as a means for protection, protection of women, protection of the oppressed, protection for those Americans victims of racial discrimination, of racism. Protecting those whom Jesus referred to as the least of our sisters and brothers.

The other beatitude, of course, is the praise of those who hunger and thirst for justice. Ruth Bader was the daughter of a Jewish migrant from Odessa, a victim of persecution who sought freedom in the United States. She grew up in the shadow of the Holocaust. She knew the persecution of the Jews, she knew the oppression of African-Americans and minorities, she knew how women had so often become victims, even of the law. She said that she took on cases so that the result would make good law.

Jews and Christians are inheritors of the covenant, God's covenant. For the Americans, so secular in their attitudes, separation of church and state, their covenant document is the Constitution. It came from the 18th century, a period of philosophy, wariness of the divine, Enlightenment, and Deism, a theism where God is in his heaven and all is well with the world. The Constitution was meant to be a Covenant with the people for dignity and freedom (with the terrible irony that some of the writers were slave owners).

Both films highlight two particular cases which Ruth Bader Ginsburg won in the Supreme Court. The first was in favour of a woman joining the Air Force, a married woman with family, but denied the benefits given to male members of the Air Force for their families. The second was in favour of a man, a widower, bringing up his children, but denied the benefits that were granted to widows on the death of their spouses in order to help them with their children's upbringing. She was a protector of women and men in issues of equality.

RBG reminds us that she was married for over 50 years to a genial husband, lawyer Marty Ginsburg, (extroverted contrast to her rather severe and humourless introverted personality), had an extraordinary personal friendship over the years with the Justice who was her complete opposite in terms of perceptions of the law, Justice Anthony Scalia. And in her old age, she became something of an icon, even jokes about her as a superhero, an inspiration. A case in point was differences in legislation about abortion, *RBG* wanting law that would allow women choice rather than be dictated to by the law.

One of the surprising things about seeing Ruth Bader Ginsburg for the first time is to see how small she was, even tiny standing next to the other Justices, not aggressive in her speeches, calmly putting a point of view, ready to put a dissenting viewpoint, but always committed to the law for the benefit and protection of all.

A Beautiful Day in the Neighborhood (2019)

Mr Rogers

JESUS NICE. Perhaps an even more surprising title than Jesus decent. The trouble with 'nice' is that it might sound too sweet, even saccharine, too nice! Although, when we come to think of it, a lot of people do say to us, 'have a nice day'. Perhaps we even say it ourselves. Probably what we mean is that we hope the day will be pleasant, easy, undisturbed.

Which is a way of introducing Mr Rogers of the United States as a Christ-figure, of Jesus nice.

Do you know Mr Rogers? Mr Fred Rogers? If we asked that question of Americans who grew up in the 1960s to 2001, they would be able to tell us immediately. He was that genial man who appeared on the television program for pre-schoolers, talking about all kinds of things – happy, serious, singing his songs, playing with his puppets, welcoming everyone to his neighbourhood. This is a tribute to him.

And here he is Tom Hanks and who is nicer on screen?

We get to know Mr Rogers through a journalist, a critical writer who is asked to do a pleasant piece about Mr Rogers as an American hero. The journalist, Lloyd (Matthew Rhys), is unwilling to meet Mr Rogers. However, conscientious, he does his job, goes to see Mr Rogers, discovers his niceness, watching him in the studio doing his television shows, having a series of interviews with him. Which don't quite turn out the way that Lloyd expected. Rather, Mr Rogers has the pleasant knack of turning back the interview,

Mr Rogers interviewing the interviewer, alert to problems, asking gently probing questions.

Mr Rogers senses Lloyd's pain, his failed relationship with his father.

Mr Rogers is able to do rather effective counselling, quietly challenging, on air as he talks so personally and intently to his audience, in his ability to interact with people.

One of the key sequences in the film is a silent minute. Mr Rogers challenges Lloyd to be quiet for a minute – and the soundtrack goes silent, we sit watching the two men. And the challenge for us is what we ourselves are doing in the silence of that minute, what are we thinking, whom are we thinking of?

One of the things that we should think of is how Jesus is presented in the Gospels, his childhood, as well as the various episodes in which he encountered children. There is not a great number but they make some significant points.

The infancy narratives of Matthew's and Luke's Gospels imagine Jesus' birth in Bethlehem, visits of shepherds and magi, the tableaus of popular cribs. But there is also the story of Jesus as refugee, fleeing persecution, living in a foreign country until it was safe to return home. And in Luke 2, there are two comments about Jesus and his growing up. In verses 39-40, 'the child grew to maturity and was filled with wisdom, God's favour was with him'. But then there is the somewhat disturbing story of Jesus, aged 12, choosing to evade his parents' supervision, stay in Jerusalem, having religious discussions with the leaders, letting Mary and Joseph search for days for him. A Bar Mitzvah story, Jesus, able to take his place in the synagogue, reading the Scriptures, coming into his own as a young Jewish man. But then the text continues (Luke 2:51-52), 'Jesus lived under their authority, increased in wisdom and stature and in favour with God'. Later Gospel references mention his family, his being the son of the carpenter – and the religious leaders taunt, asking whether anything good could come from Nazareth.

Each of the synoptic Gospels has the story of parents bringing their children to Jesus for his blessing (Matthew 18:1-4, 19:13-15; Mark 9:13-17; Luke 9:46-48). The parents had confidence in the goodness of Jesus but the immediate reaction of the disciples was to turn the children away. Jesus' reply is to let the little children come and he says that 'it is to such as these that the kingdom of heaven belongs'. He takes up this theme and asks who is the greatest in the kingdom of heaven, calling a child, setting the child in front of everyone and declaring that unless we change and be like a child we will never enter the kingdom of heaven: whoever makes themself as little as this little child is the greatest. And whoever welcomes a little child, welcomes me.

But there is the dire warning against being an obstacle to bring down 'one of these little ones who have faith'. The judgment: to be drowned in the depths of the sea, a millstone around their neck. This is a devastating judgment, especially in the uncovering of the amount of child sexual abuse in society and in the church.

And an image of Jesus gentle with a child, raising to life the daughter of Jairus, taking the little girl by the hand, 12-year-old, now alive – and solicitously recommending that they should give her something to eat' (Mark 5:35-43). Jesus also heals the son of the official who pleaded his cause, the urgency that the child was at death's door. Then the news that the child had recovered (John 4:46-54).

Jesus did introduce children into his teachings, especially in Luke 11:8-13, urging trust for prayer, asking the comic rhetorical questions about a father giving a stone instead of bread, a snake instead of a fish, a scorpion instead of an egg! Any father would never do such a thing – let alone God who answers all our prayers.

In Matthew 21:15-16, Jesus cleanses the Temple of moneychangers, heals the blind and the lame, and children cry out 'Hosanna to the Son of David' – a reference to Psalm 8:12, 'by the mouths of children, babes in arms, you have made sure of praise'. There are children also at the feeding of the 5000 – and that terrible translation of the statistic that it was 5000 men who sat down, 'to say nothing of the women and children'. At least with these references, something has been said of the children.

Mr Rogers was also a Presbyterian minister, knew the Gospels well, knew the passages about children. As has been said, *A Beautiful Day in the Neighbourhood* is a nice film in the best sense. Mr Rogers in his commitment to children is a nice man. It does make us realise that, somehow or other, we are prone to be suspicious of niceness. A pity, because we need to recognise and acknowledge it.

Radioactive (2019)

Madame Curie

A SCIENTIST CHRIST-FIGURE? But science is focused on very rational hypotheses and verification, a primacy of reason even governing scientific intuitions, laboratory experimentation – seemingly a far cry from the Jesus of the Gospels. And then there is the more than tetchy, centuries-long relationship between the church and science. It is a cliche to refer to Galileo. It is a further cliche to mention Darwin and evolution – and the challenge to the Genesis creation story. But we then remember that there is the Church of Christ, Scientist. Some scientists might be well surprised at founder, Mary Baker Eddy, and her 1879 comment that she wanted to 'reinstate primitive Christianity and its lost element of healing'. Earlier, in her book, *Science and Health with Key to the Scriptures*, she argued that sickness is an illusion that can be corrected by prayer alone. The media is prone to promote debates between those representing science and those representing religion, fostering the seeming contradictions.

However, I would like to nominate Marie Curie, Madame Curie, whose work on radioactivity spans science and healing. Within ten years of her death, Greer Garson had played her on screen in Madame Curie (1943). But, for our screen purposes, I propose *Radioactive*, 2019, featuring British actress, Rosamund Pike, as Marie Curie.

But, what is the link with the Gospel Jesus?

As Mary Baker Eddy noted in the 19th century, Jesus was a healer. He healed men, women and children in response to a great range of people interceding by prayer, for themselves, for others. It might be suggested that he did employ some methods for healing

– spitting and making a paste for blindness, urging the man born blind, John 9, to bathe his eyes in the healing waters of Siloam. But, as we know, a Christ-figure does not have to resemble Jesus in detail. It is the characteristics and qualities that are important.

Why Marie Curie can be nominated as a Christ-figure is that the trajectory of her career was from scientific investigation, intense laboratory work, the discovery of radium, of polonium (which she named after her native Poland), her initial awareness of radioactivity but, in the context of World War I, was urged (and she urged the French government) to use the developments in x-rays on the battlefields (powerful sequences in the film as she worked with her daughter, Irene, also a scientist who would win a Nobel Prize) to indicate, for instance, whether limb amputation was necessary or less dire treatments could be used. And this would lead to developments in radiotherapy, especially in the treatment of cancer.

Radioactive, it can be noted, is not solely a biography/portrait of Marie Curie. It is sometimes a visual portrait, fantasy sequences and dreams, suggestions of Madame Curie's subconscious, the contrast between her very stern manner and underlying deep emotions. This style may reflect the strong Iranian background and sensibilities of the director, Marjane Satrapi.

Rather, the film's title indicates that it is, in fact, something of a biography/portrait of radioactivity itself. Throughout the film (rather interrupting the dramatic impact of Madame Curie's life, love for her husband and their working together, his untimely death in a street accident), there are sequences that illustrate the consequences of radioactivity – flash-forwards, interrupting the drama, including the dropping of the atomic bomb, visually vivid and shocking, on Hiroshima 1945, the observing of nuclear tests in the Nevada desert in 1961, the meltdown at Chernobyl in 1986 – but also anticipation of practical applications of radiotherapy in the 1950s.

In his speech at the Nobel prize awards in 2003, Pierre Curie reminded his audience that Alfred Nobel invented dynamite and many weapons and armaments, leading him to devote his fortunes to the prizes. There were significant positive consequences but, he warned, there were dangerous consequences. And so, *Radioactive* highlights both Marie Curie herself, acclaim for her work but suffering the effects of radiation until her death in 1934.

Which means that science Christ-figures have the capacity to better our world. But there can be destructive consequences as well. And that is the challenge to the scientist.

We could say that this consideration is true for Jesus himself and his healing. We don't know the consequences for all those that he healed. The story of the healing of the ten lepers reminds us that one of the consequences is a lack of awareness in gratitude. What happened to those healed and the rest of their lives? There is a Graham Greene short story (spoiler alert for those who have not read it) where he plots the downward spiral of a man in his moral life. And then Greene reveals that this character is, in fact, the son of the widow of Naim. (I am reminded of a perceptive comment by a former confrere, John Hanrahan, that Graham Greene 'tasted life through rotten teeth'.)

Some of Jesus' actions were not without negative consequences – the choice of Judas as one of the twelve, his destructive presence amongst the disciples, his betrayal of Jesus, his final despair.

This chapter is being written in the second year of the coronavirus epidemic. Along with the other epidemic of climate change disasters, we need the best scientists (supported, as always, by prayer).

Nomadland (2020)

Fern

HAVE YOU EVER heard Jesus referred to as a nomad? Jesus Nomad? Memory tells me that I have heard him referred to as 'itinerant'. And as we come to think of it, indeed he was. He had a childhood experience of fleeing his country, refugee in a foreign land, ultimately allowed to return home. But once he left Nazareth, he spent his use of mission roaming Galilee, crossing the sea of Galilee to the Decapolis, travelling up as far as Tyre and Sidon, moving down from Galilee through Samaria, visits to Jerusalem, going out into the desert...

> Foxes have holes, the birds of the air their nests, but the Son of Man has nowhere to lay his head.

And he set a pattern for his followers. After Jesus' ascension, where the disciples were urged to go out to the whole world, Peter travelled north and then to Rome. But the arch-nomad of the early Christian times was Paul, moving, travelling widely, famous for his voyages. As we think of the church's history, nomads withdraw from society and wandered into the deserts, Francis of Assisi leaving home, begging on the roads, the extraordinary missionary journeys, Francis Xavier travelling from Spain as far as the Malay Peninsula, Japan, and the thousands of 19th-century missionaries from all churches to Asia, Africa, South America, the Pacific. There is a strong itinerant Christian tradition.

In thinking about Jesus Nomad, we have an immediate suggestion, the multi-award-winning, Oscar Best film of 2020 (a year when most of us were locked down, no nomad activity), *Nomadland*, featuring Frances McDormand who also won the

Oscar and many awards. She played Fern, an ordinary American woman, who chose to be a nomad.

Fern displays the best characteristics of a nomad, characteristics that parallel the itinerant travellers in many ways. But in the 21st-century, she does have somewhere to lay her head, her trailer, which keeps her mobile – nomads, at least in Western cultures, are not walkers but drivers. When her niece asks her if she is homeless, she replies that she is not homeless, she just doesn't have a house. And in a sense, Jesus, in the company of the chosen 12, with many disciples following at different times, with the women described in Luke 8, including Mary Magdalene significant in the group, caring for Jesus and the apostles and their practical needs.

Fern has had a tough history. Widowed, her husband dying of cancer, losing her job with the Nevada Gypsum factory as it and the town closed down, part-time teacher with a knowledge of English literature, she decides that the best place for her to be is on the road. She is a survivor. She does stop at various times, takes on practical jobs, at Amazon outlets, working on the land, a dinosaur theme park, washing up at diners, removing rubbish… But she also experiences the hospitality of the other nomads, especially some of her elderly sister-nomads.

One of the wonderful features of watching *Nomadland* is appreciating Fern, a strong character, her direct approach to life and people, yet a kindness and consideration for others, especially a capacity for listening, being a sounding board for nomads with their problems. And certainly, that was what Jesus was like on his journeys, helping, being in solidarity with those he met, listening and caring, reaching out to help.

One of the most memorable characters in *Nomadland* is Swanky, 75, diagnosed with terminal cancer, talking frankly and amiably with Fern, reminiscing about the travelling adventures of her past, of the vast cliff with swallow nests and the swarms of swallows, going on her way for more adventures until she dies, sending Fern a video of the cliff and the swallows. And Bob Wells, who manages the centre of the nomads coming and going, leading a memorial celebration of Swanky as her friends all put a stone on a cairn in her honour. It is wonderful to discover that so many of these characters, including Swanky and Bob, are not actors but actual nomads.

The other side of life for the nomads is the hospitality they receive. We can immediately think of Jesus and the disciples visiting Bethany, the welcome from the listening-attentive Mary, the fuss and busyness of Martha preparing a meal, Jesus at home with these friends. The sisters try to get in touch with Jesus the nomad when Lazarus died but Jesus was on the road, delayed, but did repay their hospitality in Lazarus's resuscitation – and the story culminating once again in a celebratory meal, hospitality.

Jesus was comfortable with hospitality. Remember the meal with a Zacchaeus, the criticisms of the scribes and Pharisees when he went to eat with the tax collectors and prostitutes, the edgy meal at the home of Simon the Pharisee when the woman who had a bad reputation in the city gatecrashed the dinner to anoint and weep, her tears washing his feet. When we look at Fern and her travels, she is able to be at home with anyone, content with her life.

It is good to be able to point to a Christ-figure like Fern, a middle-aged woman, a woman without worldly ambitions, living day by day, but showing how we, all of us, could make the best of it.

Sadly, Jesus the itinerant was cut short in his life and mission, the final walk on the way of the cross to Calvary, then his burial. But, Jesus alive, urges us all to go out and get on with our lives, living our lives to the best of our abilities. Fern is something of an everyday model.

Christ-figures, men and women together

Lorenzo's Oil (1992)

Augusto and Michaela Odone

THIS REFLECTION ON Christ-figures is not going to turn out as I anticipated. Far more complicated than I expected. It is twenty-eight years since the film, *Lorenzo's Oil*, was released and I was able to see it and review it (pleased that it had an Australian director, George Miller, and an Australian playwright, Nick Enright). I remembered the vigorous performance of Susan Sarandon as Michaela Odine and her absolute care for her young son, Lorenzo, suddenly diagnosed with a rare disease, only in boys, transmitted through their mothers. In retrospect, she seemed an obvious candidate as a mother-Christ-figure.

Suddenly, I found that the film was scheduled for a television screening. A good opportunity to be reminded. But, that is not how it turned out. Yes, there was Susan Sarandon as Michaela, absolutely dedicated, almost every waking moment, but more intensely obsessed than I recalled. Yet, the main discovery in watching the film again was how much screen time was given to Nick Nolte's Augusto, absolutely dedicated, years of commitment to studying the disease and possible paths to some kind of healing.

As I watched, it became obvious that this was a film of parental Christ-figures.

And how to reflect on this? Jesus himself was never a parent. There are some tender Gospel moments when he calls little children to him and blesses them. In fact, he tells his disciples that they must become like little children to enter the kingdom of heaven – and millstones and sea-depths for those who harm or abuse these children in any way.

In the infancy narratives of Matthew and Luke, Jesus is a child, experiencing the care of parents – refugee in Egypt, returning to Nazareth and growing in stature and maturity, obedient to Mary and Joseph.

Luke's Gospel notes twice that Mary pondered all this experience in her heart. A contemplative presence in the Nazareth household in rearing Jesus. Joseph, especially in Matthew's Gospel, is seen in the Genesis tradition of his namesake, and considered and named as a wise and just man, practical, hands-on, in the rearing of Jesus. They suggest some patterns for considering the Odines.

But there is that episode of Jesus lost in Jerusalem and his being found in the temple. Mary and Joseph search for three days, anxious, sorrowing, desperate to find him. To that extent, they may be seen as a pattern for Augusto and Michaela. For the Odones, the search for years, seemingly futile in their son's deterioration, loss of sense experience, brain damage, erratic moodiness. And the conflict with the medical profession, scientific strictures, medical trials over months, the need for funding, risks, insurance difficulties...

But the Odones persevered.

Looking again at Susan Sarandon's portrait of Michaela, there was need for reassessment. She is a dominant character. She finds it hard to brook opposition. She is dismissive – of nurses, even of her sister – if they do not measure up to her care standards. She is dismayed at the discovery that the transmission of his condition came through her, feelings of guilt continuing to eat away at her. And she is demanding on her husband. At her best, she is absolutely committed to her son.

But the interesting aspect turned out to be considering Augusto, Nick Nolte with Italian accented English, more simple in some ways, as dedicated as his wife. It is he who pursues the study, reading, investigating, discussions, theories – which, in fact, do lead to the solution, named 'Lorenzo's Oil', contributing to the developing health of many boys, preventing their collapse and suffering.

Each in their own way, Augusto and Michaela, did not give up, especially in the face of years of adversity, almost God-like fidelity.

Jesus himself encountered a number of caring parents in his healing ministry. The official, in John 4, who had such confidence in Jesus that he begged him to come and heal his son, the son recovering even while Jesus was on his way. Jairus' approach to Jesus when his daughter was dying. Jesus came to the house, touched the little girl's hand, raised her to life, was solicitous that she have something to eat. Jesus approached the widow of Naim, wept with her, restored her son to her. And there is the tenderness in Jesus' relationship with Martha, Mary and Lazarus.

And finally, John's tableau of the crucifixion, Jesus on the cross, his mother, grieving at the foot of the cross, the beloved disciple present. Jesus wants the disciple to be a son to his mother, tender care, and entrusting to the disciple to the motherly care that Jesus had experienced during his birth, his childhood, in his ministry, and now in his own care and loving concern for all, in his death.

The Railway Man (2013)

Eric and Patti Lomax

LOVE YOUR ENEMIES. Easier said, not often done.

One man who did was Eric Lomax, even though it took fifty years. He is the Railway Man (Thai-Burma Railway) of this film of a true story, based on Lomax's autobiography.

This is a film that can be recommended – with the caution that it has many harrowing moments.

The film opens with a group of aging former soldiers sitting in a veterans' club in a Scottish town by the sea. Eric Lomax is a railway man, a love for trains (as the British say, an anorak), with a seemingly encyclopaedic knowledge of the intricacies of British rail, stations, times, timetables, possibilities for connections. He suddenly rushes out of the club telling the other men that he has a puzzle to solve. It is the problem of his life, almost fifty years of PTSD, emotional blocks, nightmare memories.

A key train journey, as he misses a connection, working out another and then explaining this to the rather quiet and bemused woman passenger. They bond, his searching and finding her, a wedding. She is his wife, Patti, who is going to be the instrument of his salvation. She is a listener, a loving listener. But she is an encourager, strong, urging Eric into action which he had feared, but will become a pilgrimage to forgiveness and peace.

In the early months of their marriage, Eric has a nightmare, his adult-self back in the prison. The audience is then interned, so to speak, in that Thai-Burma prisoner of war camp, the fall of Singapore, the Japanese round-up, the cramming of prisoners on the trains, arrival at the site of the building of the railway as well as many scenes in the camp, the brutal work in the heat, the humiliation of the officers, the beatings. Eric is able to build a radio from scavenged parts which give some contact to the outside world for the prisoners. But this is short-lived and Eric is tortured. It is important that we have shared Eric's experience in the depths of its harshness so that we can appreciate the challenge to forgiveness.

When Peter asked Jesus how often he should forgive his brother or sister, seven times? Jesus replied with the perfect number, seventy times seven – always.

Older audiences who have memories of World War II, relatives who were in the camps, or have seen *The Bridge on the River Kwai*, will empathise. And we realise that Eric Lomax is very much an Everyman figure, the British man of integrity, enlisting, fighting for King and Country, taking up the cross of war and enduring its consequences.

But Eric has developed a hatred of the Japanese, a brooding hatred which has lingered and tormented him for decades. It is his version, we could say, of original sin – a need for grace that he cannot generate without help. Empathetic Patti suggests that he go on the journey that will be his salvation. He goes to Japan, but also visits the site of the camp and meets a translator there. But the healing journey brings him face-to-face with his torturer, Tagase, moments of anger and vengeance for Eric.

But then comes the challenge of Jesus, Love your enemies. The image of Jesus who had undergone agony in the garden of Gethsemane, now nailed to the cross, in his dying breath, 'Father, forgive them, they know not what they do'. What Eric has never thought of is what happened to Tagase after the war, after his brutal treatment of the soldiers in the camp. Tagase had moments of grace, acknowledged his past, changed, has devoted his life to helping others, a life in atonement. A shock for Eric but the beginning of a purging of hatred and a movement towards reconciliation. 'The hatred must stop.'

But its theme of cruelty and torture, its theme of bitterness and feelings of vengeance, its theme of asking when hatred must stop and reconciliation be fostered, make it a very moving and significant film. For all conflicts.

Eric is healed.

Boy Erased (2018)

Nancy and Marshall Eamons

OF COURSE, CHRIST-FIGURES are not perfect, but they do resemble Jesus and his characteristics in a significant way. And again, of course, the situations in which they are required to act are not perfect. The Christ-figure is an imperfect figure in an imperfect world, working to make peoples' lives better, to create a better world.

There are all kinds of social and personal situations which give rise to Christ-figures. And generally, the issue and the betterment are clear. However, there is one issue which has become less clear in recent decades, that of sexual orientation. While traditions have seen it as a moral issue, seen most frequently as a black-and-white clarity issue, the clarity is no longer there. There are issues of genetics, nature and nurture, choice, ambiguities, decisions to make transitions... It seems useful to include in this series a film which takes up the issue of sexual orientation – in a Christian context – the concern of parents, the experience of the son, and the issue of conversion therapy, presented in a Christian context.

The film is *Boy Erased*. It is based on an actual story, a Midwestern US setting (though, interestingly, written and directed by an Australian, Joel Edgerton, with Australians, Nicole Kidman and Russell Crowe playing the parents, Nancy and Marshall Eamons). Lucas Hedges plays Jared, a teenager, acknowledging his orientation, but sent by his parents to a conversion therapy program.

Antipathy towards conversion therapy will be heightened during the scenes of therapy, even the strict and stern entry into the centre, a bit like entering prison and giving up everything to be retrieved on release, filling out forms indicating defects in the family, preparing a diary of past encounters, hard role-plays with a therapist, while mouthing sympathetic and 'honest' words of feedback. It all comes across as bullying.

The parents can be seen as Christ-figures in so far as they love their son and want his betterment and peace of mind. The father, who runs a car dealership, is, in fact, a pastor in an Evangelical local church, strong views on homosexuality, condemnatory, drawing on the experience and advice of the elders of the church, inviting them to intervene with his son. The mother focuses on the love for her son, is present with him during the therapy program, serves as a loving sounding board for her son.

But there is more ambiguity in this story. Vic Sykes is a conversion therapist with convictions. His Christian presuppositions are that homosexuality is aberrant, against biblical teachings, can be fought against by therapies and the orientation reversed, 'back to normal'. The screenplay offers a critique of the therapy, whether its aims are actually achievable (temporary or permanent), the dramatisation of various sessions, the effect on the young men undergoing the program.

Which means, then, that the film is a challenge to audiences, the opportunity to reflect on their beliefs, moral perspectives, issues of sexuality, biblical and church traditions, and whether the therapy is, in fact, a catalyst for conversion.

It is frequently pointed out in such discussions that nowhere in the Gospels does Jesus speak about homosexuality. It is not an explicit Gospel issue. There are the traditions from the Jewish Scriptures, especially injunctions from the book of Leviticus. In the New Testament, there are several references to moral behaviour in Paul's letters.[1]

---

[1] There are seven texts often cited by Christians to condemn homosexuality: Noah and Ham (Genesis 9:20–27), Sodom and Gomorrah (Genesis 19:1–11), Levitical laws condemning same-sex relationships (Leviticus 18:22, 20:13), two words in

Where there is some help for considering these issues in the light of Jesus' teaching is the presentation of parents in the Gospels. There is a loving pattern of Mary and Joseph in the infancy narratives in Matthew and Luke. There is the bewilderment of Mary and Joseph at Jesus' behaviour, staying behind in Jerusalem, debating with the religious leaders, his causing them anguish in their three-day search for him.

The other main parent in the Gospels is the father of the prodigal son, the prodigal father of the parable who serves as Jesus offering an image of what God-father, God-parent, is like. We remember that the father is extraordinary in allowing his self-centred younger son to take his share of the inheritance before the right time, permitting him to go off where he lives extravagantly, even immorally, until famine hits and the young man is willing to eat pigs' slop so hungry and destitute he is. He returns, expresses contrition, and is immediately embraced by his eager father, restored to his former status, the focus of celebration, once seemingly dead, now alive.

In *Boy Erased*, Jared's mother is very much in the vein of the parable. The challenge is to his father, loving but strongly disapproving, hoping for good effect from the conversion therapy, getting authoritative religious friends to influence his son, but, ultimately, learning to listen, to empathise as far as he can with his son's experience, to acknowledge his own bewilderment, to confess his past harshness, to love while not agreeing, to be open to further loving communication.

---

two Second Testament vice lists (1 Corinthians 6:9–10; 1 Timothy 1:10), and Paul's letter to the Romans (Romans 1:26–27). The author believes that these do not refer to homosexual relationships between two free, adult, and loving individuals. They describe rape or attempted rape (Genesis 9:20–27, 19:1–11), cultic prostitution (Leviticus 18:22, 20:13), male prostitution and pederasty (1 Corinthians 6:9–10; 1 Timothy 1:10), and the Isis cult in Rome (Romans 1:26–27). Robert Gnuse, *Biblical Theology Bulletin: Journal of Bible and Culture*, 22 April 2015.

In real life, Jared's character found peace in acknowledging his orientation. Experience tells us that this is becoming more and more the reality. But for many who are caught up in the puzzle, the distress, moral issues, *Boy Erased* can be a catalyst for audiences, reflecting on the behaviour and attitudes of the parents, reflecting on the appropriateness, effectiveness of conversion therapy.

Free Guy (2021)

Guy and Milly (and Keys)

Free Guy WAS NOT ON THE SHORTLIST for Christ-figure characters, not even on a long list. And, sight immediately seen, top of the list!

A film about computer games and computer characters, the participation of the games' creators and the gamers themselves, is very contemporary. This is a film for younger generations (which, year by year, are becoming much older!). Older audiences and non-gamers would probably need a hefty tutorial, the nature of the games, the difference between characters and gamers' avatars, the goal of the games. Although, the moral of this story, voiced at the end, is that it is better to watch the characters rather than shoot them!

For audiences who watched films in the 1990s, a good comparison is *The Truman Show* where Truman cheerfully and unwittingly lives his life in a television program watched by millions, while Guy is – also cheerfully and unwittingly – living in a very popular computer game.

And probably, it is true that the gamer generation is not as familiar with Gospel stories, the characteristics of Jesus, the possibilities for Christ-figures. There is a hope that *Free Guy* might broaden horizons – although, a quick scanning of blog comments about the film shows that they are all about what a fun movie it is, only two mentioning themes of free will, life choices (and one of those thought that the screenplay was too preachy!).

So *Free Guy* and Christ-figures?

First of all, Guy. Guy is the nicest of men, happy in his routines, working in the bank, 'don't have a good day – have a great day!'. He is friends with everyone, especially Buddy, the bank security guard. There are routine robberies each day, car crashes in the street, interventions by characters wearing glasses (the avatars) and Guy's attraction towards one of them, Molotovgirl. Guy and his repetitive, day-by-day, routine is a creation of the game technicians, Millie and Keys, who have programmed his humanity so that one day, he surprises them and puts on glasses, sees everything differently, comes alive with artificial intelligence, and becomes a catalyst for change for his fellow characters, opening up possibilities for new life, free life, choices, not just accepting their taken- for-granted fate. Jesus came to give life and to give it to the full. And this becomes Guy's ambition, his mission.

In the meantime, we are continually moving between Millie and Molotovgirl her avatar, co-creator of the game, *Free City*, along with Keys, and Millie becoming the Christ-figure for Guy, so that he can have life to the full. They make quite a pair, especially as they go through all kinds of adventures together, discoveries, escaping dangers, and urging the other characters to break out of their life-pattern stereotypes – even sharing bubble-gum ice cream.

But, there is the evil genius, Antwan, CEO of the gaming company, preoccupied with money and profit, upset by the popular reception by gamers of this new Guy. We might see him as a Satan figure, a false creator, and ultimate destroyer. He targets Guy, creating another figure, a giant muscle-bound character, Dude, who resembles Guy – and who is Guy's inner alter ego, in conflict with Guy's good/nice personality. There is a moment which younger generations will relish, sounds of the *Star Wars* theme, Guy discovering a laser to fight Dude with, The Force is with him! Ultimately, Guy and his inner self make peace and are reconciled.

And we see Antwan's two assistants – Keys as a kind of good guardian Angel, committing himself to save Guy, and his collaborator, Mouser, initially a kind of bad angel but seeing through Antwan and joining with Keys and Millie to save Guy and the characters in Free City.

Which means that the filmmakers, especially the screenwriters, have relished the possibilities for inventiveness in the creation of Free City, Guy, new vision, and affirmation of life. They seem to be taking up the perennial angry accusation against God, that God should intervene whenever there are troubles and suffering in our lives. The implication is that It would seem that a God-controlled humanity would be living safe, repetitious, uninventive routines, a kind of minimal benign Fate. But life is meant to be much more than that.

It would be very interesting to listen in on a gamers' discussion about how they saw *Free Guy* and the meaning of life, having life to the full, the possibility of choices. And to hear them talking about something of the Christ-resemblances to these characters who want to create life, new life, full life.

The Year of Living Dangerously (1982)

Billy Kwan

DURING THE OPENING CREDITS of *The Year of Living Dangerously*, we are intrigued by the silhouettes, puppet outlines, light and shadow, the Wayang. Wayang is described as a dramatic representation of mythological events in a puppet shadow play or by human dancers. This drama will unfold realistically and symbolically, played by the human performers.

On the realistic level, this living dangerously year is 1965, Indonesia, the rule of President Sukarno, and the September 30 coup to overthrow him which failed. This is a story of journalists who are covering the political situation and the failed plot. On the symbolic level, the chief characters in the wayang are the Prince, the Princess, the court adviser/jester. Guy Hamilton, the incoming journalist from Australia, is to be the Prince. Jill Bryant, the Princess designate, is an assistant at the British Embassy in Jakarta. But, for audiences and for the purposes of this reflection on Christ-figures, the tantalising character is that of the adviser/jester, Billy Kwan, a dwarf, news photographer, who intervenes in the lives of both Guy and Jill.

Already there is an unusual fascination in the casting of Billy Kwan. He is played by the American actor, herself a dwarf, Linda Hunt (who won the Best Supporting Actress Oscar for her performance). She is completely convincing as Billy. We are responding to a male character, to a female performance, a character who is part-Asian, part-European, Chinese-Australian, memorable with his camera and his flamboyant tropical shirts.

Male character, female performance.

In the story, Billy becomes more than an adviser. He seems to be something of a God-figure. He seems to know everyone and everything. He has files. He has contacts (including the Communist leader). And he has plans for Guy to become his surrogate journalist, becoming aware of the enormous social problems of Asia, of the issues in Indonesia, the poverty of millions of people, and reporting honestly. And Billy will be there by his side, (a bit like God living vicariously through his creations, Billy through Guy, possessive) taking the photos, urging him on, challenging him, giving him leads, and fostering his relationship with Jill. What God might intend doesn't always happen and Billy will be disappointed that his protégés do not measure up to his expectations. Billy is dismayed by Guy's use of confidential leads for a story, feels that he has been betrayed.

But in reality, with his hopes of being the catalyst to turn Guy into a Christ-figure, Billy himself has to work in the realities of this world. And so, he becomes something of a Christ-figure himself. To begin with, like Jesus, and quoting the words of John the Baptist (Luke 3:10) as they urge repentance on them, the people respond 'What then must we do?'. Billy sees this also as the challenge to the West in the face of Asia and its needs, that the West should repent and ask what they must do.

Amongst the journalists, Billy is both respected and mocked. Many of them, however, are challenged by his moral seriousness, starting to use Gospel language about him, especially references to the crucifixion. Billy believes in his causes and is prepared to suffer for them. We see him visiting his friend with the dying child, 'I was sick and you visited me'.

However, like Jesus with some of his disciples (and echoes of Judas' betrayal), Billy is disappointed with Guy but still has some faith that he will be his better self. Injured during the uprising, Guy recalls that Billy quoted him a passage from the *Bhagavad Gita*, 'all is clouded by desire'. Guy can be redeemed. The main target of

Billy's disappointment is President Sukarno himself, whom Billy had put on a pedestal, hopeful, but disappointed in Sukarno's not responding to his country's needs. While he has praised Sukarno and trusted him, he becomes disillusioned, eventually hanging a protest banner outside a hotel, coming into conflict with the soldiers who threaten him, jostle him, tossing from the window – lying on the ground, a martyr for his beliefs. The joking journalists were not wrong about Billy's crucifixion.

AFTERTHOUGHTS

FINISHED! WONDERING HOW IT TURNED OUT... And looking back to the initial inspirations, the initial hopes.

What happened, of course, is the development while writing, choosing the Christ-figures, changes of approach, different methods. There were the continual question of how to introduce the Christ-figure in the context of the film, then when to highlight the Christ-characteristics, when to make the explicit references to the Gospels – earlier, later, how much, how little? And the making connections or leaving the readers to do this through suggestions.

The order of the Christ-figures throughout has not been in the chronology in which I wrote the chapters. In fact, *Nomadland* was the first, while *Mr Holland's Opus* was the last. It seemed better to present an objective list and to place each Christ-figure film in the order of its cinema release. This mixed the collection of men and women Christ-figures. Although there was something of a last anomaly, in the section of men and women working together, something of an exception, the male character, Billy Kwan, in *The Year of Living Dangerously*, the dwarf journalist in Indonesia, 1965, but played by an actor, Linda Hunt, who won an Oscar for this role, Best Supporting Actress. Male character, female performance.

As the writing progressed, it seemed important to check whether there was a variety of themes, a wider coverage of issues: racism, anti-Semitism, authority, leadership, justice, war and peace, the environment, sexual orientation, education, healing, serious illness, science, chaplaincy, sport, music... and ordinary men and women. But I also had to remember advice from a younger friend, making a case for younger interests in sensibilities. The Force would be with me, so some science-fiction, some young adult heroics, imaginative fantasy.

Something for the Film Buffs. The only actor to appear twice is Susan Sarandon (*Lorenzo's Oil* and *Dead Man Walking*). The only director to appear twice is Michael Apted (*Gorillas in the Mist* and *Amazing Grace*). It seemed a good idea to be patriotic and include an Australian Christ-figure (an Aboriginal, *Storm Boy* with David Gulpilil as Fingerbone). I realised at one stage: four of the directors in the final section, working on international productions, are Australian: Peter Weir, *The Year of Living Dangerously*, George Miller, *Lorenzo's Oil*, Jonathan Teplitzky, *The Railway Man* and Joel Edgerton, *Boy Erased*. Just one of those things!

This book comes from a Catholic perspective – but it is intended as ecumenical, reaching out to all Christians. And it is interfaith, reaching out to believers from different religions. And it reaches out to those who do not profess faith but who value values.

Just before writing *Mr Holland's Opus*, I was reading the book, *Jesus, An Historical Approximation*, by the Spanish writer, Jose A. Pagola (Convivial Press, Miami, 2019 (8th printing), pp. 27–28, translated so well by Margaret Wilde). He has a wonderful way of putting into inspiring words some of the thoughts and feelings I had while writing the book. Bear with me as I quote:

> First of all I have in mind Christians whom I know closely. I know how their faith can be enlivened, how much they will enjoy being believers, if they come to know Jesus better. Many of them, good women and men, live on the 'epidermis of faith', nourished by conventional Christianity. They find religious security and the beliefs and practices that are within their reach, but they do not live in joyful relationship with Jesus Christ. They have heard about him since they were children, but they are not seduced or enamoured by what they know of him. Meeting Jesus could transform their lives. I know how tempting it is to live correctly within the Church, without worrying about the one thing Jesus sought: the kingdom of God and its justice. We have to return to the roots, to the

experience that set off the long chain reaction. It does no good to confess Jesus is God incarnate, if we never try to find out what this man who revealed God to us was like, how we lived and acted...

But Jesus does not only belong to Christians. His life and message are the legacy of all humanity. The French writer Jean Onimus was right to protest: 'why should you be the private property of preachers, doctors, and a few scholars, you who spoke so simply and directly, in words that are still words of life for everyone?' As I write these pages, I was thinking of people who know almost nothing of Jesus. Men and women for whom his name has no serious meaning, or whose memory was long ago erased from their consciousness. I thought of young people who don't know much about the faith, but who feel a secret attraction to Jesus. I grieve to hear them say they have left religion for a better life. Better than with Jesus? I would rejoice if any of them found in these pages a way back to him.

I think a lot about those who have moved away from the Church out of discouragement with the Christianity they see there, and who are now looking in other directions for light and warmth for their lives...

Nothing would make me happier than knowing the good news is reaching the least of these, through means that I might never expect. They were and still are Jesus' favourites – the sick who suffer without hope, the starving, those who walk through life without love, home or friendship, women abused by their husbands or partners, those condemned to a lifetime in prison, those who feel overwhelmed by guilt, prostitutes enslaved by so many evil interests, children who have never known their parents' love, people forgotten or excluded by the church, those who die alone and are buried without a cross, those whom only God loves.

INDEED. AMEN!

www.ingramcontent.com/pod-product-compliance
Lightning Source LLC
Chambersburg PA
CBHW011317080526
44588CB00020B/2743